ADJUSTMENT
AND
TEACHER EDUCATORS

ADJUSTMENT AND TEACHER EDUCATORS

By

Ms. Pamula Praveena

M.Sc., M.Ed.

Lecturer, College of Education

Kambampadu Village

A. Konduru Mandal

Krishna District, Andhra Pradesh

Editor

Dr. Digumarti Bhaskara Rao

M.Sc., M.A., M.A., M.Ed., Ph.D.

Reader & Research Director

R.V.R. College of Education

Guntur – 522006, A.P.

digumartibhaskararao@rediffmail.com

DISCOVERY PUBLISHING HOUSE PVT. LTD.

NEW DELHI-110 002

Published by:

Namit Wasan

DISCOVERY PUBLISHING HOUSE PVT. LTD.
4383/4B, Ansari Road, Darya Ganj
New Delhi-110 002 (India)
Phone : +91-11-23279245, 43596064-65
Fax : +91-11-23253475
E-mail : discoverypublishinghouse@gmail.com
sales@discoverypublishinggroup.com
web : www.discoverypublishinggroup.com

***Reprinted:* 2019**

***First Published:* 2010**

ISBN: 978-81-8356-574-5

Adjustment and Teacher Educators

Printed at:
Infinity Imaging Systems
Delhi

Dedicated

to

Mr. **Chandra Sarat Chandra**
Mrs. **Harshitha (Chandra) Digumarthi**

in appreciation of their public-spirited services

Preface

Adjustment is a harmonious relationship of an individual to his environment which affords him comfortable life devoid of strain, stress, conflict and frustration. It consists of reactions to the demands and pressures of social environment imposed upon the individual, to which he has to react. It emphasizes the quality or efficiency of an individual where he can perform his duties in different circumstances and also emphasizes on the process by which an individual adjusts in his external environment. The adjustment process is affected and modified by the individual's experiences and thus learning plays a significant part in aiding adjustment.

Adjustment involves effective adaptation. It consists in the reduction of inner needs, stresses and strains, in this sense, adjustment could be a unique pattern depending upon the personality and the needs of the individual. As each individual differs, so his needs differ and consequently his adjustment differs. Adjustment is actually a condition or a state of mind and behaviour in which one feels that one's needs have been, or will be, gratified. The satisfaction of these needs, however, must lie within the framework and requirements of one's culture and society. As long as this happens, the individual remains adjusted; failing this he may drift towards maladjustment and mental illness.

The present study is intended to find out the adjustment of teacher educators. The teacher educators working in colleges of education are with a high adjustment. Except gender, the locality, the management of the college, the experience and the age of the teacher educators did show their influence on the level of adjustment of teacher educators and they are with high adjustment than their counter parts.

This study would be of great help to teacher educators, teacher education planners and administrators, and heads of teacher education institutions in developing proper adjustment and make the teacher education students adjust better in all avenues.

Dr. Digumarti Bhaskara Rao

Sri Sai Soudha
D-43, S.V.N. Colony
Guntur 522006
A.P., India

Contents

1

Introduction

"Life is the continuous adjustment of the internal to the external relations."

—Herbert Spencer

INTRODUCTION

Man is a social animal. He has a unique sense of belongingness to a social environment. While living as a member of social group, he comes into contact with people and situations to which he has some times to subdue and on which he has sometimes full control. His smooth living depends upon how well he can attain degree of inner harmony in his interpersonal and intrapersonal relationships. (Bhatia and Yakaiah, 2003)

The relationship which becomes established among the biological heritage or organism, the environment and the personality is adjustment. The concept of adjustment means adaptation to physical environment as well as to social demands. No human being lives apart from his physical environment. There is action and reaction chain going on between the individual and his environment. Then there are social pressures and demands of socialization. To these may be added the individual's personal demands such as physiological and psychological needs. The people who can adapt or adjust to the needs of changing condition can live happily and successfully (Bhatia and Yakaiah, 2003).

The concept of adjustment is as old as human race on earth. The process of adjustment starts from the birth of the child and continues till his death. Psychologists use the term 'adjustment' for varying conditions of social or interpersonal relationship in the society. Adjustment means reaction to the demands and pressures of social environment imposed upon the individual. The demand may be external or internal to whom the individual to react (Aggarwal, 1996).

Adjustment requires both internal and external changes. Changes in the individual's attitudes, feelings, emotions and motivations are internal adjustment. External changes are observable behaviour that are based on internal adjustments. Because of new attitudes and feelings, adjustments in outward behaviour are made. External changes include such social changes as new roles and relationships (Virginia and Quinn, 1985).

From birth to death an individual is an active organism. He is active with a purpose and his activity is continuous. He strives to satisfy not only his bodily needs but also all those other urges and drives that will enable him to function as an active member of his respective social groups. These drives follow rather definite patterns of behaviour adjustment (Crow and Crow, 1979).

A person makes efforts to adjust him some how in his environment. In these efforts, sometimes he achieves full success and sometimes only partial. On achieving partial success a person tries to find other means of adjustment (Chaube, 2002). Sometimes, he reduces his needs and as a result he may feel satisfied with in the limits of environment. He, thus, tries to maintain a balance between his needs and his capacity of realizing these needs and as long as this balance is maintained, he remains adjusted. As soon as this balance is disturbed, he drifts towards maladjustment.

"Life presents a continuous chain of struggle of existence and survival", says Darwin. The observation is very correct as we find in our day-to-day life. Everyone of us strives hard for the satisfaction of needs. In struggling to achieve something if one finds that results are not satisfactory, one either changes one's goal or the procedure. By restoring to such means one protects one's self from the possible injury to one's ego failure or frustration. It is a sort of shifting to more defensive position in order to face the challenges or circumstances after getting failure in earlier attempt or attempts. This special factor of the living organism is termed as adjustment (Mangal, 1984).

Adjustment is a signal of harmonious relationship between a man and his environment. One has to fit oneself in the prevailing circumstances. When we adjust ourselves by this means we are changing in some way to adapt or accommodate ourselves in order to fit certain demands of our environment. The conditions in the environment are in a continuous realm of changes. We change our nature in order to fit ourselves in the realm of nature. Thus the process of adjustment is a continuous one (Mangal, 1984).

Adjustment is that process through which a person tries to strike a balance between his requirements and situations (Chaube, 2002).

Some people think that adjustment involves a great deal of social conformity because, in order to survive socially, one has to become normal or like everyone else. Actually adjustment consists of two kinds of processes fitting oneself into given circumstances and changing the circumstances to fit one's needs. A good adjustment in this sense involves more than a passive relationship with one's surroundings. It involves taking the initiative, taking risks, and learning to make the most of the situation. It may even lead to an active involvement in social change. In other words, adjustment is an active and two way relationships between the individual and his or her surroundings. We try to change or modify our behaviour for bringing a perfect understanding between ourselves and our environment (Dash and Dash, 2006).

For every individual to have adjustable mentality in all aspects he should have good relationships with others because of which he turns out successfully in his social work and has good achievement too.

The individuals who are able to adjust themselves in changing or changed situations in their environment can live in perfect harmony and lead a happy life (Mangal, 1984).

Development of the personality of the child and the teacher is very much dependent on the adjustment with the environment. The efficiency of the teacher is also a great extent governed by this factor. If the adjustment is proper, there is adjustment and contentment. On the other hand, if the adjustment is not proper it leads to the development of maladjustment and discontent (Rai, 1983).

There is every necessity for the teacher educator to know about various kinds adjustments as all these adjustments together lead to a total adjustment.

STATEMENT OF THE PROBLEM

A Study of the Adjustment of Teacher Educators

NEED FOR THE STUDY

Our natural self always wants to have its own way, it in its own primitive way tends to let all our emotions have their free and unfettered expressions. On the other, our real environments, society, customs and the social way of life demand from our natural self some restraints, self sacrifices and a limited or preconceived expression. The struggle between the two opposite forces continues till it is favourably resolved and the end product is adjustment. True adjustment warrants a greater regard for environments or reality than that for the natural self because it is the reality we exist in for the whole life (Kákkar, 1989).

Now-a-days the primary concept which is missing in every individual is adjustment. Adjustment is an important issue for every individual. Adjustment decides the satisfaction level of an individual. It decides the effective ways of responding to various conditions that surround an individual.

Child is the central element of the education. The role of teacher is uncountable to draw out the potentialities of a child. For this purpose, the teacher must possess the full pledged personality. If the teacher's adjustment is perfect, then the school functioning might not matter. The teacher educator is one who plays an important role in moulding a student teacher's personality. So the teacher educator has to overcome the all the problems of adjustment. This healthy attitude of adjustment alone can achieve in bringing a healthy generations.

SCOPE OF THE STUDY

The present study is confined to the Krishna, Guntur and Srikakulam districts Andhra Pradesh State. The sample selected for the study was teacher educators, who were working in Colleges of Education and the sample size chosen for the present study was 130 teacher educators only.

The variables chosen for the study were Gender (male and female), Locality (rural and urban), Management of the college (aided and unaided), Age of teacher educators (above 45 years and below 45 years) and Experience (above 15 years and below 15 years).

The other factors that are contributing to the present study are qualification, the teacher educator's who are working in Government Colleges of Education, marital status, those working in women's colleges and co-education colleges, etc., are not taken because of time and money, and hence the researcher has confined to study to only five variables, namely, gender, locality, management of the college, age and experience of teacher educators.

OBJECTIVES OF THE STUDY

The objectives of the study were:

1. to find out the adjustment of teacher educators;
2. to compare the adjustment of men and women teacher educators;
3. to compare the adjustment of rural and urban teacher educators;

4. to compare the adjustment of aided and unaided college teacher educators;
5. to compare the adjustment of teacher educators of aged below 45 years and above 45 years;
6. to compare the adjustment of teacher educators having teaching experience below 15 years and above 15 years.

EDUCATIONAL IMPLICATIONS OF THE STUDY

The present study helps in reducing the maladjustment of teacher educators if found it in them. It also helps in adopting new conditions according to the changes in environment. If the teacher educators adopt the methods of adjustment then they will implement them in their classrooms while preparing future teachers.

2

Review of Related Literature

"If we fail to build the foundation of knowledge provided by the review of literature our work is likely to be shallow, and will be often be a duplicate work that has already been done by some one else".

—W.R. Borg

Any worthwhile research study in any field of knowledge requires an adequate familiarity with the work which has already been done in the same area. A summary of the writings of recognized authorities and of previous research provides evidence that the research is familiar with what is already known and what is still unknown and untested. Since effective research is based upon past knowledge, this steps helps to eliminate the duplication of what has been done, and provides useful hypotheses and helpful suggestions for significant investigation.

Citing studies that show substantial agreement and those that seem to present conflicting conclusions help to sharpen and define understanding of existing knowledge in the problem area, provides a background for the research project and makes the reader aware of the status of the issue. Parading a long list of annotated studies related to the problem is ineffective and inappropriate. Only those studies that are plainly relevant, competently executed and clearly reported should be included. (Bhaskara Rao, 1997).

Capitalizing on the reviews of expert researchers can be fruitful in providing helpful ideas and suggestions. While review articles that summarize related studies are useful, they do not provide a satisfactory substitute for an independent research. Even though the review of related literature is not a substitute for an independent work, it is one of the first steps in the research process. It is a valuable guide to define the problem, to recognize its significance, to suggest promising data gathering devices, to appropriate study design and sources of data for effective analysis and to arrive at fruitful conclusions. (Bhaskara Rao and Kumari, 2000).

The need and importance of related studies and literature have been highlighted by Best, who says that "Particularly all human knowledge can be found in books and libraries" unlike other animals that most start a new with each generation, man builds upon the accumulated and recorded knowledge of the past.

Dewey has outlined review of related studies as the third step of the scientific method. It is a crucial step which invariably minimizes the risk of dead ends, rejected topics, rejected studies, wasted efforts, trail and error activity extended towards approaches already discarded by previous investigations and even more important erroneous findings based on the faulty research design.

The survey of related literature and studies also helps to avoid the risk of duplication. It helps the investigator to see whether the evidence already available solves the problem adequately without further investigation, thus to avoid the risk of duplication.

Though the search for related literature is a time consuming process, it is necessary for a good research. Hence, this chapter i.e. Reviews of Related Literature, is meant for the study of adjustment of teacher educators.

THEORETICAL PERSPECTIVES

Here, the theoretical concepts related to adjustment will be viewed clearly so as to have a clear idea about adjustment.

I. Meaning of Adjustment

Herbert Spencer introduced the term 'adjustment' into scientific parlance in his principles of Biology in 1864. Various concepts of adjustment depend upon the meaning that it read into the word 'satisfactory' or what constitutes a satisfactory relationship (Rao, 1990).

Originally, the meaning of adjustment was borrowed and changed from the concept of "adaptation" in biology. Adaptation refers to the biological changes that facilitate the survival of a species. At the psychological level, adjustment means the individuals' struggle to survive in his or her surroundings (Dash and Dash, 2006).

The dictionary meaning of the word 'Adjustment' is to fit, make suitable, adapt, arrange, modify, harmonize or make correspondent (Mangal, 1999).

The concept of adjustment means adaptation to physical environment as well as to social demands. The word 'adjustment' in its ordinary sense means the arrangement of different parts of a thing, say an instrument, into their proper places so as to ensure harmony in its working. Here the word has been used with reference to the emotions of man which need to be adjusted (Kakkar, 1989).

According to Gilmer, we can think of adjustment as psychological survival in much the same way as the biologists use the term adaptation to describe psychological survival.

The concept of adjustment was originated by Darwin who used it as adaptation to survive in the physical world. If we observe human beings we find that their behaviour develops as a reaction to a variety of demands or pressures that are brought to bear upon them in their physical environment. The biological concept of adaptation was borrowed by psychologists and renamed it as adjustment (Cauhan, 1983).

The different responses, behaviour and expressions of a person towards a situation is called 'adjustment'. In short, it can be said that an organism's behaviour is governed by his wishes and desires and that different forms of behaviour are outcome of different forms of wishes as well needs (Tiwari, 1984).

Adjustment has two meanings. In one sense, it is a continuous process of life which an individual effects changes in his behaviour. He also tries to keep his proper relationship with the environment. In the second sense, adjustment is that conductive situation in which an individual keeps himself happy and free from mental ailments.

Adjustment is dependent on the following factors, viz., internal power of the individual and proper and conductive environment.

When both these things are present, there is adjustment.

II. Definitions of Adjustment

"Adjustment means the modification to compensate for or meet special conditions." (James Drever, 1952)

"Adjustment is the establishment of a satisfactory relationship, as representing harmony, conformance, adaptation or the like." (Webster, 1951)

"Adjustment is the process of finding and adopting modes of behaviour suitable to the environment or the changes in the environment." (Carter V. Good, 1959)

"Adjustment refers to any operation where by an organism or organ becomes more favourably related to the environment or to the entire situation, environmental and internal." (Warren, 1934)

"Adjustment is the process by which a living organism maintains a balance between its needs and the circumstances that influence the satisfaction of these needs." (Shaffer, 1961)

"Adjustment is a continual process in which a person varies his behaviour to produce a more harmonious relationship between himself and his environment." (Gates and Jersild, 1948)

"Adjustment as psychological survival in much the same way as the biologist uses the term adaptation to describe physiological survival." (Geuner, B. Vonhaller, 1970)

"An individual's adjustment is adequate, wholesome or healthful to the extent that he has established harmonious relationship between himself and the conditions, situations and persons who comprise his physical and social environment." (Crow and Crow, 1956)

"Adjustment is the interaction between a person and his environment. How one adjusts in a particular situation depends upon one's personal characteristics as also the circumstances of the situation. In other words, both personal and environmental factors work side by side in adjustment. An individual is adjusted if he is adjusted to himself and to his environment." (Arkoff, 1968)

"Adjustment is the outcome of the individual's attempts to deal with stress and meet his needs also, his efforts to maintain harmonious relationships with the environment." (James C. Coleman)

"A good adjustment is one which is both realistic and satisfying. At least in the long run, it reduces to a minimum the frustrations, the tensions and the anxieties which a person must endure." (H.C. Smith)

"Occasionally in the use of the term 'adjustment' we imply that the most desirable state of adjustment is one in which the individual is perfectly happy and satisfied with all aspects of his life and one in which he has reached the level in all his contacts with his environment that he would be glad to see and persist through his life." (Traxler)

"Adjustment is harmonious relationship with the environment involving the ability to satisfy most of one's needs and meet most of the demands, both physical and social that are put upon one." (*Dictionary of Behaviour Science*)

"A state of life when the individual is more or less in harmony with personal, biological, social and psychological needs and with the demands of the physical environment."

"Adjustment is a state in which the needs of the individual on the one hand and the claims of the environment on the other hand are fully satisfied or the process by which this harmonious relationship can be attained." (Eyesenk)

"Adjustment as a process involving both mental and behavioural responses by which an individual strives to cope with inner needs, tensions, frustrations, conflicts and to bring harmony between these inner demands and those imposed upon him by the external world." (Shaffer and Shoeben)

"In growing cultures, the effective people do not adjust to the environment but instead adjust the environment to suit their needs." (John Dewey)

"Adjustment is a process and not a state. Adjustment is continuous throughout life." (Ruth Strang, 1949)

"Adjustment is a satisfactory relation of an organism to its environment." (Symonds, 1933)

III. Nature of Adjustment

The nature of adjustment of an individual is governed by biological factors as well as upon his social experiences which he receives in his environment. Adjustment has a multidimensional nature. The concept of adjustment was originally biological one and was concerned with adaptation to physical environment for survival. Adaptation to physical environment is, of course, a person's important concern, but he has also to adjust to social pressures and demands of socialization that are inherent in living interdependently with other persons. There are also the demands from a person's internal nature his physiological needs like hunger, thirst, sleep, sex, elimination, etc., and psychological needs like to belong to get esteem, to self- actualize, to get in combination and in interactive fashion that influence the psychological functioning and adjustment of the person (Aggarwal, 1996).

Although the actual nature of the personal adjustment of individual will become clearer as the discussion moves forward with a few preliminary suggestions that may be useful in viewing the individual task.

First, the individual adjusts actively in the school environment rather than passively adjusting to the school's programme. When a learner enters a class, he does something to that group, just as the group does something to him. This concept of dynamic interaction between the individual and the group has roots both in modern interpretations of the learning process, this view fits nearly also with the democratic philosophers' insistence that each individual shall count as a contributor to his society as well as a recipient of the benefits of sharing in the life of the group.

Second, we do not mean here by adjustment as any unhealthy twisting of one's personality through withdrawing from others evading responsibility or deceiving oneself, however much comfort may come there from, rather, we have seek under the title "adjustment" healthy, energetic participation in group activity, grasping of responsibility, at times to the point of leadership and above all, avoidance of any self deception in the adjusting.

Third, since the personality of the individual so largely is a product of learning adjustment is essentially a process of relearning, although a variety of factors influence adjustment directly or indirectly.

Adjustment has both negative and positive aspects. From the negative side, the elimination or reduction of emotional maladjustment is sought, where as from the positive side, the focus is open healthy and realistic, ways of thinking and acting since adjustment is not a peculiar, mysterious, psychological trick.

IV. Characteristics of Adjustment

As per J.C. Aggarwal (1996), the characteristics of adjustment are:

1. Adjustment helps us to keep balance between our needs and the capacity to meet these needs.
2. Adjustment implies changes in our thinking and way of life to the demands of the situation.

3. Adjustment gives us the ability and strength to bring desirable changes in the state of our environment.
4. Adjustment is physiological as well as psychological.
5. Adjustment is multidimensional.
6. Adjustment brings up happiness and contentment.

V. Elements in Adjustment

The adjustive behaviour or adjustment (Parameswaran and Beena, 1988) implies the following:

1. There must be a need on the part of the individual to adjust.
2. There are some situations or circumstances which render some forms of behaviour more adjustive than others.
3. The individual must have the ability or capacity to behave in an adjustive manner.
4. This adjustive behaviour should result in an effective adjustment, thus bringing to a termination the demand for adjustment.

An analysis of the process of adjustment will reveal the presence of the following main elements (Sharma, 2004).

1. Motive

The very process of adjustment in the living being is set in motion by the presence within him of some motive or need or requirement.

2. Thwarting Condition

When the environment does not present any features that tend to become obstacles in the fulfillment of these needs, then the adjustment is natural facile and effortless and no problem results. But, if circumstances create obstacles in the path of such fulfilment then the process of adjustment progresses further.

3. Varied Responses

Once the fulfilment of a need has been obstructed, the individual indulges in various actions which are a reaction to the obstacle. Such a reaction can be normal just as much as it can be abnormal.

4. Solution

As a result of these reactions and responses, the individual achieves a degree of adjustment with the circumstances. The problem of adjustment is there by solved.

VI. Criteria of Adjustment

Certain criteria have been evolved to assess the adequacy of adjustment of an individual in his environment.

1. Psychological Comfort

One of the most compelling signs of adjustment failure is that a person is psychologically uncomfortable in some way. Discomfort may include state of depression, acute anxiety, obsessive thought of guilt or fear of illness, etc. Experiencing discomfort often implies some inadequacy of psychological adjustment.

2. Work Efficiency

Another sign of adjustment difficulties is impaired ability to make full use of social capacities.

3. Physical Symptoms

Some times, the only evidence of inadequate adjustment appears in the form of damage to body tissues.

4. Social Acceptance

Some kinds of adjustment are socially acceptable, that is, they are what other persons want.

Norman Talent has suggested the following criteria for good adjustment.

1. Good Subjective Feeling

A well-adjusted person must be free from neurotic fears and anxiety and must feel psychologically comfortable. The individual sees a meaning in his life.

2. *Personal and Social Achievement*

The individual should be able to develop his potentialities to the maximum. He should be able to achieve self-actualization. He should establish good relation in the society in conformity with the norms of the society.

3. *Ability to Work*

Adjustment refers to performance physical and mental work satisfactorily in accordance with one's capacity.

Criteria of Personality Adjustment

Adjustment means harmony in a person's needs, wishes and his circumstances. On the basis of adjustment it is easy to judge a person's personality as well as behaviour. Psychologists have provided some of criteria. They, as per Tiwari (1984), are:

1. *Balance of Personality*

Personality is the sum total of various traits. As such, the main criterion of personality adjustment is a balanced personality. There is uniformity in the emotions, desires, etc., of a well adjusted personality.

2. *Decrease of Tension*

Decrease of tension is availed in an adjusted personality. When a person's needs and desires are not satisfied, he develops mental tension within and when they are satisfied, his tension decreases and he gets adjusted. As such, on the basis of decrease of tension in an individual, it can be known whether the individual is adjusted or not.

3. *Harmony between Need and Environment*

An individual's adjustment depends on the harmony between his needs and his environment. The more the harmony, the better the adjustment. A person's adjustment to his environment depends on the (a) the extent of harmony between an individual's drives, motives, etc., (b) the extent to which an individual's wishes as well motives are satisfied, and (c) the extent to which his desires, needs or behaviour is governed by the social norms.

4. Competence in Interpersonal Relations
5. Emotionally balanced, free from Conflicts and Frustrations
6. Physical Health

The individual should be free from physical ailments like headache, ulcers, indigestion and impairment of appetite. These symptoms in individual have some times psychological origin and may impair his physical efficiency.

VII. Areas of Adjustment

Adjustment in case of an individual should consist of personal as well as environmental components. These two aspects of adjustment can be further subdivided into smaller aspects of personal and environmental factors. Adjustment, although seeming to be a universal characteristic or quality may have different aspects and dimensions.

Arkoff (1968) in his book *Adjustment and Mental Health* has enumerated the family, school or college, vocation and marriage as the important areas of adjustment.

Joshi (1964) and Pandey, in their research study covering school and college students, have given 11 areas or dimensions of an individual's adjustment:

1. Health and physical development
2. Finance, living conditions and employment.
3. Social and recreational activities
4. Courtship, sex and marriage
5. Social psychological relations
6. Personal psychological relations
7. Moral and religious
8. Home and family
9. Future - vocational and educational
10. Adjustment to school and college work
11. Curriculum and teaching

The main areas of adjustment (S.K. Mangal 1999) are the following:

1. *Health Adjustment*

One is said to be adjusted with regard to one's health and physical development and abilities are in conformity with those of his age mates and he does not feel any difficulty in his progress due to some defects or incapabilities in his physical organs and he enjoys full opportunity of being adjusted.

2. *Emotional Adjustment*

Emotions play a leading role in one's adjustment to self and his environment. An individual is said to be emotionally adjusted if he is able to express his emotions in a proper way at a proper time. It requires one's balanced emotional development and proper training in the outlet of emotions.

3. *Social Adjustment*

How far one is adjusted can be as curtained by one's social development and adaptability to the social environment. Social adjustment requires the development of social qualities and virtues in an individual. It also requires that one should be social enough to live in harmony with one's social beings and feel responsibility and obligation towards one's fellow beings, society and country.

4. *Home Adjustment*

Home is the source of greatest satisfaction and security to its members. The relationships among the family members and their ways of behaviour play a leading role in the adjustment of a child. All problematic and delinquent behaviours are the result of that adjustment and just maladjustment, to a great extent, is the product of faulty rearing and uncongenial atmosphere at home.

5. *School or Occupational Adjustment*

The school environment casts its influence over the adjustment of the children and the adolescents. How far a child is satisfied with his school building, its discipline, time table, co-curricular activities, methods of teaching, class and schoolmates, teachers and head of the institution is completely in the pattern of this total adjustment.

The occupational world of adults dominants the mode of adjustment, degree of satisfaction with the choice of occupation, working condition, relationship with colleagues and boss, financial satisfaction and chances for promotion decide one's adjustment to occupation and contributes significantly towards one's overall adjustment (Mangal, 1984).

Adjustment of a person is based on the harmony between his personal characteristics and the demands of the environment of which he is a part. Personal and environmental factors work side by side in bringing about this harmony.

VIII. Need and Goals in Adjustment

A need is a state of tension in the person which tends to direct his behaviour towards goals which will relieve the tension. A goal is an activity which satisfies the need. On the other hand, a situation or a work that fulfils the need of a person is called a 'goal'.

The needs of the person may be divided into two categories primary or physical needs and subsidiary or psychological needs.

Primary needs are those without whose fulfilment it is difficult to a man to survive. If they are not fulfilled, the question of fulfillment of subsidiary needs does not arise at all. Sometimes, subsidiary needs also assume the place of primary needs.

That primary needs are physical needs and the secondary needs are psychological needs. It does not mean that psychological needs do not have physical basis. The basis of psychological needs is also physical. The only difference is that it is difficult to analyze and explain the physical basis of the psychological needs.

Psychological needs are also called social needs. They are termed so because they grow out of the conflict with the society.

It is quite possible to call physical needs as social needs and social needs as bodily needs.

1. Physical Needs

The physical needs are include eating, air, normal temperature, rest, sleep, etc., on which the life of a person depends. These things are also called life security needs. Good taste, sweet music, beautiful articles are some more examples.

2. Psychological Needs

The various psychological needs of the personality are not so important as the basic needs. But they do play an important role in life. They are:

(i) Need for love and affection

(ii) Need for society

(iii) Need to achieve success

(iv) Need for freedom

(v) Need for social appreciation or acceptance by society

(vi) Emotional needs (Rai, 1983).

IX. Process of Adjustment

Man differs from others on the basis of his intellect. Through his intelligence, he is able to cope with his needs as well with his environment. His harmony between his needs and his environment is termed as adjustment. The adjustment of man starts from motivation. A person's mental mechanism is effected by the origin of motives and as a result he gets inclined to activity. He activates in such a manner so that his motives can be satisfied. But every motive cannot be satisfied due to several internal as well as external barriers. As such he tries in one way or the other and when his motives are satisfied, he feels relief.

This adjustment process of an individual's mental life attains satisfaction and this individual feels adjustable with his environmental situations.

1. Adjustment as an Achievement and as a Process

Adjustment may be viewed from two angles. From one angle, adjustment may be viewed as an achievement or how well a person handles his conflicts and overcomes the resulting tension. From another angle, adjustment may be looked upon as a process or how a person adjusts to his conflicts (Aggarwal, 1996).

Adjustment as a process describes and explains the ways and means of an individual's adaptation to his self and his environment without reference to the quality of such adjustment or its outcome in terms of success or failure.

2. Continuous Process

The process of adjustment is continuous. It starts at one's birth and goes on without stop till one's death. A person as well as his environment is constantly changing as also are his needs in accordance with the demands of the changing external environment. Consequently, the process or terms of an individual's adjustment can be expected to change from situation to situation and there is nothing like satisfactory or complete adjustment which can be achieved once and for all time. It is something that is constantly achieved and re-achieved by us.

Adjustment is a two-way process and involves not only the process of fitting oneself into available circumstances but also the process of changing the circumstances to fit one's needs (Mangal, 1999).

3. Adjustment as a Psychological Process

Adjustment, as a process, is of major interest to psychologists who want to understand a person and his behaviour. The way one tries to adjust himself to his external environment at any point of time depends upon the interaction between the biological factors in growth and his social experiences.

There are three broad types of adjustment process in the event of a conflict between a person's internal needs and environmental demands. They are: (a) The person may modify or inhibit the internal impulse. (b) The person may try to alter the environmental demand in some manner so that he resolves the conflict. (c) The person may escape through unconscious resources to mental mechanisms like phantasy, compensation, projection, rationalization, sublimation, etc. (Aggarwal, 1996).

X. Determinants of Adjustment

The determinants of adjustment can be classified into biological and cultural. The quality of adjustment in an individual depends upon his ability to establish harmony between himself and his environment. In adjustment, the two crucial factors are the individual and the environment. When we try to study the individual, we have to take into consideration the hereditary and biological factors, the physiological factors and the quality of socialization given to him.

1. The Biological Determinants

The biological determinants of adjustment have their roots in the heredity of the individual. Each individual is unique from the biological point of view because his genetic background is unique and it determines his potentialities.

According to James C. Coleman:

> "At conception, each new individual receives a genetic endowment from his parents which provides for the physical equipment, muscles, glands, sense organs, nerves and so on essential for his development into an adult human being. The specific characteristics of this equipment, of course, vary widely from one individual to another. Thus, heredity not only provides the potentialities for development but is an important source of individual differences."

From the above, it is quite clear that heredity provides the basic structure for development and adjustment of the individual. If the biological structure of the individual is defective, he is bound to develop problems of adjustment.

The biological determinants of adjustment are also related to the biological needs of the individuals. According to James C. Coleman, the following four biological needs are most relevant in terms of human motivation and adjustment: (1) Viscera for food, water, oxygen, sleep, the elimination of wastes and other substances and conditions necessary for life. (2) Safety relating to the avoidance of bodily harm or damage. (3) Sex basic to the perpetuation of the species and important to individual fulfilment. (4) Sensory and motor for sensory stimulation and motor activity in order for bodily equipment to develop and function properly.

These biological needs provide motivation for human behaviour and they must be satisfied by the individual keeping in view his culture and environment.

2. *The Cultural Determinants*

The cultural determinants of adjustment are important because they permit the individual to adjust within the framework of cultural norms, values and standards of behaviour. Among the cultural determinants of adjustment mentioned may be made of: (1) Family structure; (2) Education in the school; (3) Social organization; (4) Sub-cultural loyalties-social and political; (5) Economic condition; and (6) Caste, class, racial and religious harmony.

There are cultural determinants which are related to the socialization and acculturation of the individual. In other words, the way a person is brought up by his parents and the quality of relationships which he later develops determine his adjustment. (S.R. Jayaswal, 1964)

XI. Characteristics of a Well-adjusted Person

A well-adjusted person is supposed to posses the following characteristics (Mangal, 1999).

1. *Awareness of his own Strengths and Limitations*

A well-adjusted person knows his own strengths and weaknesses. He tries to make capital out of his assets in some areas by accepting his limitations in others.

2. *Respecting Himself and Other*

The dislike for oneself is a typical symptom of maladjustment. An adjusted individual has respect for himself as well as for others.

3. *An Adequate Level of Aspiration*

His level of aspiration is neither too low nor too high in terms of his own strengths and abilities. He does not try to reach for the stars and also does not repent over selecting an easier course of his advancement.

4. *Satisfaction of Basic Needs*

His basic organic, emotional and social needs are fully satisfied or in the process of being satisfied. He does not suffer from emotional cravings and social isolation. He feels reasonably secure and maintains his self-esteem.

5. *Absence of a Critical or Fault Finding Attitude*

He appreciates the goodness in objects, persons or activities. He does not try to look for weaknesses and faults. His observation is scientific rather than critical or punitive. He likes people, admires their good qualities, and wins their affection.

6. *Flexibility in Behaviour*

He is not rigid in his attitude or way of life. He can easily accommodate or adapt himself to changed circumstances by making necessary changes in this behaviour.

7. *Capacity to Deal with Adverse Circumstances*

He is not easily overwhelmed by adverse circumstances and has the will and the courage to resist and fight odds. He has an inherent drive to master his environment rather than to passively accept it.

8. *A Realistic Perception of the World*

He holds a realistic vision and is not given to flights of fancy. He always plans, thinks and acts pragmatically.

9. A Feeling of Case with his Surroundings

A well-adjusted individual feels satisfied with his surroundings. He fits well in his home, family, neighborhood and other social surroundings.

10. A Balanced Philosophy of Life

A well adjusted person has a philosophy which gives directions to his life while keeping in view the demands of changed situations and circumstances. The philosophy is centered on the demands of this society, culture, and his own self so that he does not clash with his environment or with himself.

XII. Methods of Adjustment

According to Mangal (1999), the methods used for keeping and restoring harmony between the individual and his environment can be grouped into two categories, viz., direct methods and indirect methods.

1. Direct Methods

Direct methods are those methods which are employed by the individual intentionally at the conscious level. They are rational and logical and help in getting permanent solution of the problem faced by the individual in a particular situation. These methods include the following.

(a) Increasing Trails or Improving Efforts

When one finds it difficult to solve a problem or face obstacles in the path, to cope with his environment he can attempt with a new zeal by increasing his efforts and improving his behavioural process.

(b) Adopting Compromising Means

For maintaining harmony between his self and the environment one may adopt the compromising postures such as: (i) he may altogether change his direction of efforts by changing the original goals; (ii) he may seek partial substitution of goal; and (iii) he may satisfy himself by an apparent substitute for the real thing.

(c) Withdrawal and Submissiveness

One may learn to cope with one's environment by just accepting defeat and surrendering oneself to the powerful forces of environment and circumstances.

(d) Making Proper Choices and Decisions

A person adapts himself to, and seeks harmony with his environment by making use of his intelligence for the proper choices and wise decisions particularly when faced with conflicting situations and stressful moments.

2. Indirect Methods of Achieving Adjustment

Indirect methods are those methods by which a person tries to seek temporary adjustment to protect himself for the time being against a psychological danger. There are purely psychic or mental devices-ways of perceiving situations as he wants to see them and imaging those things that would happen according to his wishes. That is why these are called defense or mental mechanisms employed in the process of one's adjustment to one's self and the environment. A few mental mechanisms are: (a) Repression; (b) Regression; (c) Compensation; (d) Rationalization; (e) Projection; (f) Identification; (g) Seclusiveness or withdrawal; and (h) Sympathism.

According to Sharma (2004), every individual has certain definite needs, and every individual lives in certain specific conditions. It is within these conditions that his needs are fulfilled when the conditions are favourable, no particular difficulty arises in such fulfilment, but for every individual this is not always possible. A condition that is not propitious for the fulfilment of some need is not in the life of every individual and such circumstances and conditions always prove obstacles in the satisfaction of that needs thus creating problems. Difficulties refer to the conditions that prove obstacles to the satisfaction of a person's needs. As it is, one finds great individual differences in the manner of reacting to these difficulties, but even then there are certain modes of reaction that can be seen in every pattern of reaction behaviour. These methods are the following:

1. Constructive Adjustment

One very general form of reaction to difficulties is the mode of constructive adjustment, and examples of this mode of behaviour are to be seen in everywhere in life. When a trader is faced with some problems of his trade, he resorts to some constructive adjustment to solve the problem.

In constructive adjustment, the main feature to be remarked is that it offers a quality of facing the situation rather than running away from, and of making efforts to solve the problem instead of merely postponing it.

2. Substitute Adjustment

All individuals do not have the ready wit and wisdom to achieve constructive adjustment and thus retain their mental balance in the face of difficulties. A very large number of individuals have recourse to substitute adjustment when faced with difficult situations. This also is a common and usual method of reacting to the difficulties. These reactions are activities of adjustment, since they do not tend to solve the problem inherent in the situation. A close observation will reveal that even through such reactions the individual is trying to satisfy needs that in other individuals are solved through constructive and positive adjustment activity. When tensions that are created through the obstruction, he tries to end by his activity of running away or transferring the blame on to the teachers or by day-dreaming of success. Thus, for this reason are these reactions to difficulties called substitute reactions.

On the other hand, these modes of adjustment are also usually harmful for the individual. One characteristic of proper and constructive adjustment is that not only the individual but the entire society benefits from it, besides improving the individual and social relationships.

3. Mental Mechanism

Another mode of reacting to difficulties is that of mental mechanisms, main among them being projection, compensation, rationalization, etc. As a general rule, the consequence of these mechanisms is not good either for the individual or for the society. Yet, in some degree or other, all or some of these mechanisms are to be found in every individual, hence no individual can be declared abnormal on their account. These mechanisms are called the tools of adjustment through various methods.

4. *Adjustive Reactions*

Adjustive reactions, as is evident from the name are those reactions that achieve an adjustment between the individual and his circumstances. In this manner, constructive adjustment reactions are included in adjustive reactions. As a general rule, the simplest method available to a person to satisfy his motives when conditions exist to frustrate them is to redouble his efforts to achieve his satisfaction and to do so with patience and persistence.

On the other hand, there are other individuals who avoid a condition of stress and conflict by controlling emotions and motives in a manner that leads to a reasonable adjustment and compromise with circumstances. One very important feature of adjustive reactions is that it benefits the individual organism as well as the community organisms, or at least is not harmful to such a community.

5. *Partially Adjustive Reactions*

All reactions aimed at facing obstacles so as to satisfy motive are not completely and entirely successful in achieving their objective. Some of them succeed only in attaining a partial adjustment. Some partial and temporary adjustment of a kind is definitely achieved by this escapist dreaming, but no individual can get complete happiness through this kind of imaginative adjustment. Evidently, reactions of this kind do not achieve any considerable adjustment.

6. *Non-Adjustive Reactions*

Non-adjustive reactions as a class are activities that do not achieve any adjustment at all between the individual and his conditions. For instance, some people do not attend to some motive even when it is persistently and continually being frustrated. And they continue in activities that do not bring satisfaction for this motive. When this happens, some people, instead of doing something to satisfy it, only choose to repress it all the more, but the efforts at repression and suppression are only non-adjustive reactions as they achieve no real adjustment at all.

7. *Mal-Adjustive Reactions*

These activities or reactions do succeed in achieving some adjustment, but a type of adjustment that is of a wrong kind it harms the individual organism as well as the community of organisms. This class of reactions includes all kinds of adjustive mechanisms or mental mechanisms. Besides a person who finds at dissatisfaction in the achievements of other individuals by identifying himself with them gives some appearance of being adjusted, but he neither himself progresses nor does he afford assistance to others in their progress and development. Society glares at and vociferously criticizes people who have recourse to maladjustive reactions, and ultimately it causes them pain and discomfort.

XIII. Theories or Models of Adjustment

According to Mangal (1999), there are several theories and models describing the pattern of adjustment. Some of the important models are explained here under:

1. *Moral Model*

This represents the oldest view point about adjustment or maladjustment. According to this view, adjustment or maladjustment should be judged in terms of morality, i.e., absolute norms of expected behaviour. Those who follow the norms are adjusted and those who violate or do not follow these norms are maladjusted. Evil supernatural forces like demons, devils, etc., were blamed for making one indulge in behaviour against the norms (committing sins) while the religious gods, goddesses and other saintly great souls were responsible for making one a happy, healthy, prosperous and pious person (adjustive in modern sense). However, as the medical and biological sciences advanced and scientific reasoning gained a firm footing in the nineteenth century, the moral model was replaced by the medico-biological model.

2. *Medico-Biological Model*

This model holds genetic, physiological and biochemical factors responsible for a person being adjusted or maladjusted to his self and his environment. Maladjustment, according to this model, is the result of a disease in the tissues of the body, especially the brain. Such a disease can be the result of heredity or damage acquired during the course of a person's life by injury, infection, or hormonal disruption arising from stress, among other things. In the opinion of Lazaras (1976), the correction of adjustive failures or disorders requires correction of the tissue defects through physical therapies such as drugs, surgery and the like.

This model is still and enjoys credibility for rooting out the causes of adjustive failure in terms of genetic influences, biochemical defect hypotheses, and disease in the tissues of the body. However, it is not correct to assign physiological or organic causes to all maladapted and malfunctioning behaviour, especially when there is no evidence of physiological malfunction such a situation certainly calls for other explanations, views, points or models.

3. *Psychoanalytical Model*

This model owes its origin to the theory of psychoanalysis propagated by Sigmund Freud (1938) and supported by psychologists like Adler, Jung and other neo-Freudians.

(a) Freud's Views

In the Freud's system of psychology and psychoanalysis, we have to see those factors which are relevant to success or failure in adjustment.

1. The human psyche or mind consists of three layers, the conscious the sub-conscious and unconscious. The unconscious holds the key to our behaviour. It decides the individual's adjustment and maladjustment to his self and to his environment. It contains all the repressed

wishes, desires, feelings, drives and motives many of which are related to sex and aggression. One is adjusted or maladjusted to the degree, extent or the ways in which these are kept dormant or under control.

2. According to Freud, man is pleasure seeking animal by nature. He wants to seek pleasure and avoids pain or anything which is not keeping with this pleasure loving nature. The social restrictions imposed by the mores of society and his own moral standards dictated by his super ego come in conflict with the unrestricted and unbridled desires of his basic pleasure seeking nature. These pleasures are mostly sexual in nature. One remains adjusted to the extent that these are satisfied. An individual drifts towards malfunctioning of behaviour and maladjustment in case such satisfaction is threatened or denied. Freud postulated the imaginary concept of 'id', 'ego' and 'super ego' for the adjustive and non-adjustive behaviour pattern and formulated the following conclusions:

   A person's behaviour remains normal and in harmony with this self and his environment to the extent that his ego is able to maintain the balance between the evil designs of his id and the moral ethical standard dictated by his super ego. In case the ego is not strong enough to exercise proper control over one's id and super ego, malfunction of behaviour would result. Two different situations could then arise:

   (a) If the super ego dominates then there is no acceptable outlet for expression of the repressed wishes, impulses and appetites of the id. Such a situation may give birth to neurotic tendencies in the individual.

   (b) If the id dominates, then the individual pursues his unbridled pleasure seeking impulses, without care for the social and moral norms. In such a situation, the individual may be seen to be engaged in unlawful or immoral activities resulting in maladaptive, problem or delinquent behaviour".

3. Freud also uses the concept of libido, i.e., a flow of energy related to sex gratification. He equates it with the flowing river and maintains that:
   (a) if its flow is outward causing sex gratification and pleasurable sensation from outside objects, the individual remains quite normal and adjusted to his self and environment.
   (b) its inward flow leads to self-indulgence and narcissism.
   (c) if its path is blocked, this results in its arrest leading to regressive behaviour, a kind of abnormality.
   (d) if the flow of the libido is dammed up, condemned or repressed through the authority exercised by the ego in association with the super ego, it may cause severe maladjustment. When the ego is weak and the super ego is rigid this may lead to psychotic personality disorders. However, when the ego is weak and the super ego also is not too rigid it may result in relatively simple disorders like neurosis or still simpler maladaptive behaviour characterized by restlessness, sleeplessness, head ache, stomach ache, back ache vomiting, lack of appetite, etc.
4. According to Freud, adjustment or maladjustment should not be viewed only in terms of what the individual may be undergoing at present and what happened to him in his earlier childhood is even more important. What he may have experienced as a child, what types of gratification to his sex urge he has achieved, what has been repressed in his unconscious, how he has passed through the distinct stages of sexual development, etc., are thus, quite important for making him adjusted or maladjusted to his self and the environment.

(b) Adler's Views

Adler disagreed with his teacher, and substituted the sex motive with the power motive or desire to attain superiority and perfection to explain human behaviour. He maintained that:

1. There is an inherent strong urge in all human beings to seek power and attain superiority. Besides this as a child, one is helpless and dependent, which makes one feel inferior and in order to make up for the feelings of inferiority, one takes recourse to compensatory behaviour, i.e., indulges in a struggle for power. Environmental situations, constitutional deficiency and many other factors may also make one feel inferior and to get away from these feelings one learns to struggle for achieving power. An individual's efforts for seeking power or attaining perfection may also be the result of his need for creative expression, the urge to do something new, to enhance his status in the eyes of his colleagues and others.

2. Stimulated thus by the urge to seek power or attain superiority and perfection, one adopts a distinctive life style suited to one's environmental situations. One continues to strive for superiority by emulating and exploiting the ways and means provided by one's life-style. Adjustment or the lack of it would depend on whether one's efforts end in success or failure to achieve one's goal. Thus, the following three stimulations may arise:

   (a) Success in seeking gratification of one's power motive or attaining superiority may lead to good adjustment to one's self and the environment.

   (b) In case of partial failure, if one is successful in bringing about a slight modification in one's life's goals or style of life one may be able to reconcile with one's self and the environment and may feel adjusted and remain normal.

   (c) In case of failure to obtain gratification of the power motive and to changing one's goal or style of life, one may drift towards non-adjustive or maladjustive behaviour leading to mild or severe mental illness.

(c) Jung's View

Jung's system of analytical psychology advocated the idea of the 'self-actualization motive' instead of Freud's 'sex gratification motive' and Adler's 'power seeking motive' for explaining the way and how of human behaviour. According to him, one has a strong inner urge or motive to exhibit one's talents or abilities or seek self actualization. Accordingly, one utilizes one's life energy, i.e., the flow of libido as a channel for self-expression to satisfy the urge for self-actualization. The degree of adjustment of one's personality depends on the extent to which one is successful in actualizing oneself. Libido, the life energy, as Jung maintains, may flow both ways inward and outward, turning an individual into an introvert or extrovert personality. In the introvert, thinking is predominant while sensations and feelings are suppressed. In the extroverts, on the other hand, the feelings or sensations are more predominant and the thinking in is suppressed. Generally speaking, however, an individual is neither purely introvert nor a purely extrovert. He is ambivert, i.e., while showing the symptoms of an introvert, he possesses some characteristics of the extrovert and *vice versa*. As long as a person can maintain proper balance between his thinking and feeling he remains adjusted to this self and environment. But, lopsided behaviour i.e., laying too much emphasis on thinking at the cost of feelings or giving too much consideration to feelings at the cost of thinking may disturb the balance of one's psyche. It may lead to maladaptive behaviour causing mild or severe mental illness.

Another criterion for normal or properly adaptive behaviour, according to Jung's theory, is the reconciliation between one's conscious and unconscious behaviour. Failure on one's part to maintain or achieve such reconciliation may lead to maladaptive behaviour and mental illness. When one's conscious is not in true with the unconscious or when the unconscious turns hostile on account of being not properly understood by the conscious it is bound to create imbalances in one's mind and make one's behaviour quite hostile to one's self and to one's environment. If this hostility or aggression is directed inward, one becomes neurotic but when it over flows outwards, one turns into psychotic delinquent character. In some severe forms of insanity, as claimed by Jung, we find a complete autonomy of the unconscious, a type of complete control or bombardment of the conscious mind by the unconscious contents in the shape of disturbing and unusual ideas. Harmony or discord between one's conscious and unconscious may thus proves to be a deciding factor for one's personality to be termed as adjusted or maladjusted to one's self and the environment.

The views of other neo-Freudians and later psychoanalysts and the other followers of the psychoanalysis school also tried to put forward their own view points explaining the way and how of human behaviour. Notable among them were Karen Horney, Erich Forman, Wilhelm Rich and Erik H. Erickson. Let us briefly discuss their views.

(d) Karen Horney's Views

While Adler thought the need for power (to counter the feelings of inferiority) to be the root cause of human behaviour, Horney (1937) placed emphasis on the need of security (to offset the feelings of anxiety). She postulated that an individual as a child feels helpless and isolated in a potentially hostile world. This creates some basic feelings of anxiety and the craving for security in him. A reasonable concern with security is normal. But, if an individual is obsessed with security to the exclusion of self development, he is likely to drift towards maladaptive or abnormal behaviour.

The anxious child, she further theorizes, may ultimately move towards people and become dependent upon them, move against people and become hostile and rebellious, or move away from people and withdraw into himself. If a person can integrate these three attitudes or responses, some times giving, sometimes fighting and sometimes keeping to himself, he may remain adjusted to his self and his environment. But in case he turns too much to one of these directions, regardless of the appropriateness in specific circumstance, he is bound to become maladjusted ending up with mild or server mental illness or delinquent behaviour.

The other reason for maladjustment, according Horney's theory, may be the denial or obstruction in the way of realizing one's need for self-esteem or self-realization. Anxiety is the result of situations where one starts by not valuing one self highly enough. A conflict then arises between one's ideal self and the real self. An individual can remain adjusted and normal to the extent that the balance between these two selves is satisfactorily maintained and may drift towards abnormal or maladaptive behaviour if this is disturbed.

(e) Erich Fromm's Views

Like Horney Fromm also emphasizes the need of security and feels that as a child one may feel the necessity for belonging to offset the fear of isolation and aloneness. Consequently, the individual in his childhood may desire to live in the family, belonging to the members of the family and provided with love, affection and security by them. In due course, however, when he attains maturity he is impelled by an inner craving for freedom and as a result he tries to escape from the very bonds which provided him the security he needed. In this kind of situation he may be confronted with the inner conflict of being dependent for the satisfaction of this need of security and his urge for freedom. This conflict is further heightened when parents and other members are also caught in the situation in the form of allowing independence to their progeny to play their roles as mature persons or trying to hold them back as a guarantee of their own future security. The extent to which this crisis of dependence verses independence or security verses freedom is resolved by the children with the help of their parents and elders, governs the degree to which their behaviour and functioning remain adjusted and normal. In case this crisis is not resolved satisfactorily, maladjustment and maladaptation followed by mental illness and delinquent character formation may result.

(f) Wilhelm Reich's Views

In agreement with Freud's views on the importance of sexuality, Reich firmly believed that an individual's health both physical and psychological depends on the liberation of the sex drive, all the way to orgasm. However, from the day of birth, the release of libido or sexual energy is blocked by parents, teachers and society in general. Reich considers the term sexual energy in a wider connotation calling it organ energy, a life force emerging the total behaviour of an individual and responsible for all types of self expression. If this energy is properly channelized and flows along normal and natural ways, the individual remains adjusted and enjoys good physical and mental health. But, in case the flow of this energy is blocked it may lead first to somatic or physical discomfort and then to the physiological and psychological disorders leading to mild or severe maladjustment and mental illness.

(g) Erickson's Views

This contemporary psychologist of the twentieth century views adjustment as a function of the conflict between inborn instincts and societal demands. He has divided the entire human life span into eight distinct stages. At each stage, the society characterized by a particular culture puts up a specific demand which may or may not suite the urges or instincts manifested at that specific stage by the individual. In this away, at each stage of life, one is faced with the crisis. The resolution of which can have either a good or bad effect on one's adjustment. For example, during the stage of infancy, the individual is confronted with the problem of resolving a crisis peculiar to this stage, i.e., trust (enabling him to form intimate relationships) verses mistrust (enabling him to protect himself in the hostile world) for this proper growth and development. The outcome of his behaviour depends upon the success or failure of the satisfactory resolution of this crisis and consequently he may grow into a wholesome healthy personality or a defective and deviant personality.

4. Sociogenic Model or Cultural Model

According to this model, the society in general and culture in particular affect one's ways of behaving to such an extent that behaviour takes the shape of adaptive or maladaptive behaviour turning one into an adjusted or maladjusted personality. A society and culture to which one belongs does not only influence or shape one's behaviour but also sets a standard for its adherents to behave in the way it deserves.

Individual behaving in the manner that desires are labelled as normal and adjusted individuals while deviation from social norms and violation of role expectancy is regarded as the sign of maladjustment and abnormality. Although, society or culture plays a significant role in shaping and influencing human behaviour, yet it should not be regarded as the only factor in the adjustment process. More over, the societies or cultures may themselves, rather than the individual be maladaptive and sometimes even descriptive to the individuals' adjustment like Nazy Germany. It is not proper, therefore, to depend solely or the sociogenic or cultural model for the labeling of one's behaviour as adjusted or maladaptive.

5. *The Socio-Psychological or Behaviouristic Model*

The socio-psychological or bahaviouristic model in general emphasizes that:

1. Behaviour is not inherited. Competencies required for successful living are largely acquired or learned through social experience by the individual himself.
2. The environmental influences provided by the culture and social institutions are important but it is the interaction of one's psychological self with one's physical as well as social environment which plays the decisive role in determining adjustive success or failure.
3. Behaviour, whether normal or abnormal is learned by obeying the same set of learning principles or laws. Generally, every type of behaviour is learned or acquired as an after-effect of its consequences. The behaviour one's occurred, if reinforced, may be learned by the individual as normal. As a result one may learn to consider responses which are labeled normal, or abnormal.
4. Not only is normal and abnormal behaviour learned, the labeling of behaviour as normal or abnormal is also learned. Whether or not an individual is considered abnormal or maladjusted for a particular type of behaviour depends upon the observation of the behaviour and also upon the social context of the behaviour.

5. Maladaptive behaviour may be treated by applying the principle of behaviour modification, and learning, deconditioning and correcting environmental situation responsible for its occurrence.

XIV. Measurement of Adjustment

Measurement as an instrument of inquiry is now frequently used in behavioral sciences. At a general level of classification in behavioral science, the following five different types of measuring techniques are used:

1. Testing techniques;
2. Projective techniques;
3. Inventory techniques;
4. Sociometric techniques; and
5. Scaling technique.

In the area of measurement of adjustment, inventory techniques are the most popular because they have many advantages compared to her techniques. Testing techniques can only be used to assess the characteristics of individuals at the conscious and projective techniques only at the unconscious level. The adjustment behaviour, the adoption to changed circumstances involves both conscious as well as unconscious behaviour. Therefore, the two techniques separately are unable to give a proper assessment of an individual's adjustment.

Sociometric techniques are used in the measurement of social relationships. They can provide clues to the level of social adjustment. Social adjustment is only one part of an individual's total adjustment. The other aspects of his adjustment like psychical, mental, emotional, social and occupational are not explored by the sociometric techniques and they can not, therefore, be used for the accurate assessment of an individual's total adjustment.

In scaling techniques, opinions are collected from some other person or persons about the adjustment pattern of a particular individual known to the respondents. Adjustment as a wide phenomenon carries so many things with it that one cannot judge the adjustment pattern of another individual from his over behaviour and the inner private world or reactions of an individual cannot be assessed by the use of scaling techniques.

Some important inventories and measures of adjustment are:

1. Bell's Adjustment Inventory developed by Hugh M. Bell.
2. Edward's Personal Preference Schedule (EPPs) published by Psychological Corporation, New York
3. The Heston Personal Adjustment Inventory developed by Joseph E. Heston.
4. The Mooney Problem Checklist.
5. Asthana's Adjustment Inventory developed by H.S. Asthana.
6. *Vyaktitva Parakhs Prashnavali* developed by M.S.L. Saxena
7. Sinha's Adjustment Inventory developed by A.K.P. Sinha and R.P. Singh.
8. Joshi's Adjustment Inventory developed by M.C. Joshi and Jagadish Pandey.
9. Adjustment Inventory for Older People devised by P. V. Ramamurthi.

XV. Maladjustment

Maladjustment refers to the failure of the individual to adjust to the needs of self and demands of the environment.

Adjustment or maladjustment is inferred from the behaviour an individual shows in a given situation. Behaviour that is in conformity with the demands and expectations of others, peers, teachers, parents, siblings and community members is called adaptive behaviour. Behaviour that fails to meet the social and cultural patterns is called maladjustive behaviour.

The term 'maladjustment' has two aspects, viz., emotional disturbance and social maladjustment. Although social maladjustment and emotional disturbance in people are not necessarily synonymous, there is a considerable overlap between them. Social maladjustment refers to behaviour of people which is not within the range of the culturally permissible either at home, in the school, or in the community. These people are unmanageable in the home, causing difficulties for the parents and siblings. In the community they may seek undesirable comparisons or be isolates. Delinquents are subgroup of the socially maladjusted.

The term 'emotionally' disturbed refers to those who have inner tensions and show anxiety, neuroticism or psychotic behaviour. Emotional disturbance does not always cause social maladjustment. For example, the isolate or withdrawn may be considered emotionally disturbed but not come in conflict with the lives of others.

Socially, maladjusted people are usually emotionally disturbed, but not always. Similarly emotional disturbance may lead to social maladjustment, but not always. Social maladjustment may lead to delinquency but not always. But, all delinquents have some forms of social maladjustment. It appears when that maladjustment may first appears as emotional disturbance when maladjustment leads to aggressive behavior, stealing, or destruction of property and causes conflict with the law, such an individual is called a delinquent, Thus the three levels of maladjustment are emotional disturbance, social maladjustment and delinquency.

Dennis (1972) holds a similar view point. He states:

> "when emotional handicaps react the stage of being so grave as to affect social development leading to the behaviour disorder and frequently influencing school work, we term this maladjustment".

Health Service Regulations of 1945 suggests what

> "maladjustment is exemplified by pupils who show evidence of emotional instability or psychological

disturbance and requires special educational treatment in order to effect their personal, and educational readjustment".

1. *Signs of Maladjustment*

The Underwood Committee, London (1955) set out six groups of symptoms commonly associated with maladjustment. Examples of these six groups of symptoms are:

(a) Nervous disorders

Fears and anxiety, marked solitariness and timidity, depression and obsession, excitability and apathy, hysteria and amnesia.

(b) Habit disorders

Speech defects and stammering (other than those caused by physical defect), excessive daydreaming, sleeplessness and nightmares, facial and body tics, nail-biting, rocking, bed-wetting and physical symptoms such as asthma and allergies.

(c) Behaviour disorders

Temper tantrums, destructive, defiant or cruel, stealing, lying, truancy; sex aberrations.

(d) Organic disorders

Neurological dysfunction, head injuries, brain tumors, epilepsy.

(e) Psychotic disorders

Hallucinations, delusions, bizarre behaviour.

(f) Educational and Vocational Difficulties

Lacking concentration, unable to hold down a job, irregular response to school discipline, slow learning, retarded in recording particularly.

The appearance of any of the symptoms does not of itself signify maladjustment. These symptoms may not be also necessarily permanent. These symptoms range from mild to severe and many mild cases can be dealt within the normal school setting by teachers.

Maladjusted behaviour is to be judged in terms of a society's existing standards. Thus, what is commonly acceptable to a society at one time might be thought of as quite unacceptable at another time. Again changes in attitude as a result of the process of maturity should not be taken as signs of maladjustment. Adolescents in search of adult standards, values and privileges may appear to some parents to be suffering from behaviour disorders, where as, in fact, the onset of these attitudes is a healthy developmental sign.

2. Causes of Maladjustment

There is no single factor which causes maladjustment among children and people. The causes of maladjustment are many and varied. Again some children are predisposed to maladjustment. That is to say, some children tend to be easily maladjusted under certain situations where as other do not. The causes of maladjustment can be grouped under three heads:

(a) Psychological factors;

(b) Psychosocial factors; and

(c) Physiological Factors.

(a) Psychological Factors

Maladjustment is very often caused by life's frustrations. When a child is placed in situations in which his capacities are strained, or in which he is unable to satisfy his motives and drives, behaviour deviations of aggression, regression, compulsive behaviour or other abnormal reactions may result. Maladjustment is the outcome of frustration resulting from the discrepancy between the child's capacity to behave and the requirements of the environment. Maladjustment is common among children whose parents are over ambitious or expect too much of them without due regard for their capacities.

(b) Psychosocial Factors

Not all maladjustments arise from frustrations in an immediate situation or from the discrepancy between the child's capacity to behave and requirements of the environment. Other factors include early experiences and social and economic aspects of the child's environment.

Different types of maladjustment are caused due to specific home situations. Some children defy all authority, are hostile towards authority figures, are cruel, malicious, and assaulters and have inadequate guilt feelings. Such children are jealous, deceitful and blameful of others. Such children are known as unsocialized aggressive children.

There are some children who are known as socialized aggressive. Such children are aggressive and hostile to authority figures, but they are socialized within their peer groups, the gang or companions. Maladjusted children also fall into a third category called over inhibited. They lack close friendships, are over dependent and easily depressed. They have frequent physical complaints.

The three categories of maladjusted children and their home background indicate that maladjustment is caused at home by such factors as over protection, rejection, hostility and inconsistent discipline.

(c) Physiological Factors

Just the mind has effect on the body, so also the body has effect on the mind. Neither psychological factors nor the psychosocial factors explain all forms of maladjustment. There may be some physiological factors which might have caused maladjustment.

3. Remedial Measures

Just as there is no single cause of maladjustment, so also no one can prescribe a ready made solution to the problems of maladjusted children. Maladjustment may be caused due to multiple causes. The remedies also depend upon the collaborative effects of a number of persons, teachers, guidance workers, psychologists and health officers.

Maladjustment may be mild or severe. It may appear in the form of emotional disturbance, social maladjustment or delinquency. The remedy also can vary from mental health practices in the regular schools to treatment in residential schools.

The teacher is not among professional personnel to deal with maladjusted children. Remedial measures for maladjustment fall under the sphere of psychologists and psychiatrists. But the teacher can do a lot to help the maladjusted child live a happier life in the school and overcome some of his difficulties. Here we will only mention the specific measures the teacher can take to help the maladjusted children:

1. The teacher should try to understand the cause behind the defiant behaviour of the child.
2. He should try to certain the seriousness of the problem by studying the symptoms of maladjustment.
3. He may educate the parents about effective child rearing practices and healthy relationship between parents and their children.
4. He must ensure that the atmosphere in the school, interpersonal relationships between the teacher and the child, teacher's expectations and behaviour patterns, quality of teaching, etc., are all conductive to the well being of the child.
5. The teacher, in collaboration with his colleagues, should adopt good mental health practices in the school.
6. He should refer the child to appropriate professional personnel per treatment, if the child is found not curable in the regular school programmes.

XVI. Defence Mechanisms

Life is largely a process of satisfying needs and desires. Needs give rise to goal oriented behaviour in an organism. Obstacles in the path of need fulfillment lead to frustration. Frustration produces worries and anxieties. It is not easy for an individual to face frustrations and solve conflicts, he, therefore develop certain mechanisms to defend his ego and keep his feeling of security undamaged. It has been mentioned by W.K. Benton and A.E. Benton that:

"A frustration which seems to a person to show that he does not measure up to his picture of himself (his ego-ideal) is said to be ego-involving. Some psychological mechanisms are attempts to protect one against ego-involving frustrations. These are called defense mechanisms."

There are certain psychological devices which an individual uses in order to protect himself from the damaging effects of ego-involving frustrations. It may be noted here that psychological devices used by an individual to protect him against ego-involving frustrations are not only known as defense mechanisms but they have other names as well. These are mental mechanisms and adjustment mechanisms. Thus in order to escape the effects of frustrations, an individual may use those psychological devices which have been described as defense mechanisms, mental mechanisms and adjustment mechanisms. The difference is only in name but not in their nature and function.

1. *Meaning of Defence Mechanisms*

"Defence mechanism is any enduring structure of the psyche that enables a person to avoid awareness of the unpleasant or anxiety - arousing." (English and English)

"When psychological equilibrium is threatened by severe emotional traumata, frustrations, or conflicts, the mind resorts to a variety of protective subterfuges and detours called mental mechanisms of dynamisms." (Jame D. Page)

"Adjustment mechanisms are the habits by which people satisfy their motives, reduce their tensions and resolve their conflicts." (Shaffer and Shaben)

"Ego defense mechanism is a type of reaction designed to maintain the individual's feelings of adequate and worth rather than to cope directly with the stress situation; usually unconscious and reality distorting." (James C. Coleman)

"From the very outset the ego has to try to fulfill its task of acting as an intermediary between the id and the external world in the service of the pleasure principle, to protect the id from the dangers of the external world. In this battle, on two fronts the ego makes use of various methods of fulfilling its task, i.e., to put it in general terms, of avoiding danger, anxiety and displeasure. We call these devices defensive mechanisms." (Sigmund Freud)

2. Characteristics of Mechanisms

The characteristics of defence, mental or adjustment mechanisms are:

1. Defence mechanisms are unconscious methods which a person uses.
2. Defence mechanisms are used in order to avoid anxiety.
3. According to Page, mental mechanisms are 'forms of self deception" and the individual making use of them is not aware of either their presence or purpose.
4. Defence mechanisms are used even by normal persons in moderation with a view to making adjustment.
5. In their exaggerated forms defence mechanisms are indicative of mental abnormality. According to Page, when defense mechanisms become ends in themselves they are to be taken as abnormal symptoms.
6. Defence mechanisms when used in excess, distort realities of life and the individual making use of them feels secure in a world of fantasy.
7. Defence mechanisms give relief from tensions and anxiety and that is the main purpose behind their use.
8. A person making excessive use of defence mechanisms develops feelings of inferiority and insecurity and lacks self confidence.
9. Defence mechanisms are not acquired deliberately. Defence behaviour develops through blind learning and does not involve conscious choice.

3. Types of Mechanism

There is no agreement among psychologists in regard to the types of mechanisms. Nevertheless an easy approach to classify defence mechanisms may be in terms of various types of reactions to frustrations. On the basis of different types of reactions defense mechanisms can be classified into the following three categories:

(A) Withdrawal Reactions

(B) Aggressive Reactions

(C) Compromise Reactions

A. *Withdrawal Reactions*

Among withdrawal reactions the following types of defence mechanisms are included:

1. Fantasy

Fantasy enables the individual to reduce his frustrations by withdrawing from the painful and real situations. Some individuals indulge too much in day dreaming and fantasy because they cannot face the problems of life. Thus fantasy is a kind of defense mechanism.

2. Dissociation

Dissociation is the inability of the individual to perceive the association between an action and its consequences. Further, dissociation may assume the form of compulsive behaviour a person is unable to perceive and understand the meaning of his behaviour, with the result that he goes on repeating it.

3. Nomadism

Nomadism refers to withdrawal from an unpleasant location or place. Some times an individual feels that a particular place of town is responsible for his frustrations because in that town the source of his frustration is located. Hence he tries to move away from that place. This has been termed as nomadism. Nomadism may also occur if the case of frustration is lack of ability or there is some kind of motivational conflict within the individual. So, he goes away from the place and returns to it many a time.

4. Repressions

Repression is that kind of withdrawal reaction in which certain motives are repressed or forgotten. Through forgetting, one may escape the pains of frustrating situation. It has been stated in this connection that repression as a withdrawal reaction should be considered equal to forgetting. But, it should not be equated with such forgetting as are caused by the loss of memory or due to some other serious loss leading to it.

5. Reaction Formation

When a person drawn towards socially undesirable objectives and goals he may try to repress this factor by doing such things as well indicate that he was not striving for undesirable goals. If some one says that he was not pursuing socially undesirable goals he will protest it. The reason for this protest is that the individual is not conscious of his repression. Nevertheless, the reaction formation type of withdrawal is indicative of the unconscious desire for a socially undesirable object and at the same time the individual concerned may be against it openly.

B. Aggressive Reactions

Under this category of defence mechanisms, the following are included:

1. Displaced Aggression

Displaced aggression is that mechanism which prompts a person to do something as a substitute for something else. This substitution is known as displacement. Sometimes some individuals do not find any substitute for their aggression. In such cases, suicide is committed. Suicide is that kind of displaced aggression in which an individual substitutes himself for expressing his anger.

2. Projection

Projection is another type of aggressive reaction. In this defense mechanism, an individual tries to ascribe his own faults to other people. Through projection one may reduce this feeling of guilt.

C. *Compromise Reactions*

Defense mechanisms under this category of compromise reactions are mainly four:

1. Sublimation

The defense mechanism of sublimation has been described by Freud. It relates to the efforts when a person tries to modify his socially undesirable motives. It has been said that all art is a kind of sublimation of sex feelings, urges and desires.

2. Compensation

Compensation is another type compromise reaction. As a defense mechanism it may be used by a person who has been unsuccessful in one direction or pursuit. In order to maintain the frustration due to lack of success, the individual may try some other object or pursuit. It was Alfred Adler who very much emphasized the role of compensation as a defense mechanism. A student, who is not good at studies, may try to compensate this lack by becoming a good sportsman.

3. Identification

Identification as a compromise reaction in the form of a defense mechanism enables an individual to feel satisfied by identifying himself with the achievement of others. In other words, with the help of the mechanism of identification, a person tries to think the success achieved by some other person to be his own. Thus what he was not able to achieve at the conscious level, he achieved it through identification at the unconscious level.

4. Rationalization

Rationalization is another type of compromise reaction. As a defense mechanism, it enables the individual to minimize his faults and he may unconsciously play down his frustrations. A typical example is provided by the saying that the grapes are sour.

D. *Classification of Mechanisms*

It was stated by Adeline Detach that every aspect of personality has a kind of defense mechanism against anxiety.

For example, intelligence may be used as a kind of defence mechanism. Likewise, dominance and submission in different individuals also function as defense mechanisms.

According to P.M. Symonds, "the classification of mechanisms has presented considerable difficulty and no classification scheme is fully satisfactory." Likewise, Shaffer and Shoben have also accepted the difficulty in classifying adjustment mechanisms.

In order to classify different defense mechanisms, a survey of the indexes of eight books on adjustment and mental hygiene published between 1945 and 1950 was made. This survey revealed that in these eight books thirty two different types of adjustments or defense mechanisms were mentioned. Another interesting fact that was discovered was that only two mechanisms were mentioned in all the eight books. The mechanisms of identification, projection and regression were mentioned only in seven books. Mechanisms of aggression, compensation, fantasy and negativism were mentioned only in six books. The remaining twenty three mechanisms were discovered only in one to four books.

The results of this survey quite clearly emphasized the complexity involved in the classification of defense mechanisms. Every author has taken his own position. It is, therefore, desirable for us to consider the classification of defense mechanisms by some prominent authors of books on adjustment and behaviour disorders.

A. *Symond's Classification*

P.M. Symond's has presented different mechanisms under the following groupings:

1. Repression (the exclusion of an impulse from consciousness) and inhibition (the blocking of discharge or expression of an impulse).
2. Escape from conditions which might arouse expression of the impulse.
3. Disguise of the true meaning and significance of the uninhibited expression of the impulse.

4. Modification of the expression of the impulse.
5. Payment of a penalty for the forbidden expression
6. Autoerotism.

B. Cameron's Classification

Norman Cameron used the term adjustive techniques instead of defense mechanisms. According to him, adjustive techniques are those habitual methods which human beings in our society use in overcoming, avoiding, circumventing, escaping from or ignoring frustration and threat.

Cameron has further emphasized that these 'adjustive techniques' are simply ways of manipulating situations and reducing the tensions of need and anxiety, of suspense, the wasting and conflict. They are certainly not, as at one time believed, primordial forces, well springs of psychic energy. Justifying the use of his term adjustive techniques in place of 'defense mechanisms", Cameron writes - "Psychopathologists of the nineteenth century introduced the terms "Mental mechanisms", "Psychic mechanisms" and "Dynamisms" to designate certain of these adjustive operations under the naire impression that they were describing psychic entities instead of human behaviour.

From the above it is quite clear that Clemson considers different adjustive techniques basically patterns of human behaviour keeping in view the above view point, the following classification of different adjustive techniques by Cameron should be studied:

(A) General Adjustive Techniques

In the category of general adjustive techniques, Cameron has included direct aggression and tempers tantrum and simple withdrawal, fear and anxiety.

(B) Special Adjustive Techniques

According to Cameron, the acquisition, development and use of special adjustive techniques differ greatly from person to person. Nevertheless, they can be reduced into two groups of five adjustive methods.

Cameron has further emphasized the fact that these special adjustive techniques are not mutually exclusive. They overlap and each one of them may have characteristics common with others.

In the first group of special adjustive techniques are included those methods which Cameron described as 'defense techniques' because they defend the ego of the individual. These defense techniques are attention getting, identification, compensation, rationalization, and projection.

The second group of special adjustive techniques has been termed as 'escape techniques' because their main purpose is to enable the individual to withdraw and escape from a situation of anxiety and stress.

(C) Shaffer's Classification

Shaffer and Shoben used the term adjustment mechanisms and defined it as "the indirect or substitute habits of adjustment". This is in a narrow sense the meaning of adjustment mechanism as suggested by Shaffer and Shoben.

They further stated that substitute adjustment mechanisms are to be found among all people because everyone has to face some kind of frustration and make efforts to resolve them or reduce tension through some substitute adjustment mechanisms.

Commenting on the uses of substitute mechanisms, Shaffer and Shoben stated that "they serve useful purposes in integrative. The study of mechanisms is valuable for the understanding of human nature in general, as well as for the treatment of conduct disorders."

Thus adjustment mechanisms are valuable not only for maladjusted persons but also for normal people. This fact is one of the great discoveries of modern psychologists.

Shaffer and Shoben, while recognizing the difficulty involved in classifying adjustment mechanisms suggest that adjustive responses can be conveniently grouped into five types of adjustment mechanisms. These are given below:

1. Adjustment by Defence

In this category, all those mechanisms are put which are mainly aggressive or outgoing. It has further been stated by Shaffer and Shoben that mechanisms of this category "usually involve some group interaction or communication, but of an antisocial and non-integrative nature, such mechanisms have been described as moving against people".

2. Adjustment by Escape

Under this category, all those mechanisms, that are basically based on withdrawal type of responses are included. These mechanism make the individual "more away from people".

According to Shaffer and Shoben, adjustment by escape mechanisms is characterized by lack of social activity, passive seclusiveness and satisfactions derived from living in fantasy.

3. Adjustments Involving Focal Fears

Under this category, all such adjustment mechanism are included which have the factors of fear or anxiety in their focal points. Different types of phobias and irrational fears are included in this category.

4. Adjustment by Ailments

Certain physical illness such as paralyses and pain in body are a kind of adjustment mechanisms which a maladjusted person may try to use. They are to be found mostly among neurotics.

5. Anxiety States

The fifth and final category of adjustive responses is mainly due to deep seated anxiety within the individual. According to Shaffer and Shoben, "the anxiety states are mainly non-adjustive. They are not mechanisms that reduce tensions but are evidences of unresolved adjustment problems."

In Shaffer and Shoben's classification, we find that adjustment mechanisms take into account the various types of adjustive responses in terms of moring against people and moring away from people they further take into account the various types of neurotic ailments which are nothing but unconscious efforts on the part of the individual to reduce tension and find peace. Nevertheless such adjustive responses and efforts do not help the individual in tension reduction. They require psychiatric treatment.

The above discussion about various aspects concerned to adjustment will make everyone understand well the adjustment.

RESEARCH STUDIES

The researcher has traced a few researches done in the past that have a little relevance to the present study.

1. Adjustment and Gender

Gupta, Sushma (1990) found that:

- adolescent girls studying in co-educational schools were significantly better in their social adjustment as compared to adolescents of girls schools.
- adolescent girls studying in English medium schools were significantly better in their social adjustment as compared to girls of Hindi medium schools.
- education of father and education of mother positively influenced the social adjustment of adolescent girls.
- parents of girls studying in urban and English medium schools had a better opinion regarding the social adjustment of their daughters as compared to the parents of girls in rural and Hindi medium schools.
- adolescent girls studying in urban, private co-educational and English medium schools belonging to the higher SES showed better social adjustment.
- adolescent girls studying in urban schools were significantly better in their social adjustment as compared to girls in rural schools.

- adolescent girls studying in private schools showed significantly better social adjustment as compared to those of government schools.

Baral (1969) reported that ill adjustment was observed among boys but not among girls, difference between boys and girls within groups were not seen.

Mehta, et.al. (1988) found that there was not much difference in the adjustment problems between the boys with superior scholastic ability and the boys with average scholastic ability.

Shirotriya (1988) found no difference in marital adjustment among Hindu and Christian males and females, but a significant difference was found between Muslim males and females. Males and females differed in marital adjustment on the basis of religiosity.

Gaur (1988) found no significant difference among the problems of male and female teacher educators.

Mankad (1982) states that ill adjustment was observed among adolescent boys but not among adolescent girls.

Singh (1982) found that adolescent girls with high and low achievement have differential adjustment pattern.

Kasinath (1991) found that:

- Hindi and Non-Hindi speaking boys did not differ significantly in respect of their emotional and educational adjustment.
- Hindi and Non-Hindi speaking boys differ significantly in respect of their social adjustment.
- HS and NHS girls did not differ significantly in respect of their emotional, social and educational adjustment.
- HS boys and NHS girls did not differ significantly in respect of their total adjustment.
- HS girls and NHS boys did not differ significantly in respect of their total adjustment.

Subrahmanian (1989) stated that elderly males and females differed significantly in perception of support, adjustment, role activity, involvement and satisfaction.

Rather (1990) found that:

- boys as well as girls differed significantly in their adjustment.
- boys showed more adjustment difficulties in comparison to girls.
- girls were found socially better adjusted than boys.

Shah (1989) found that:

- family climate was found to be effective in case of urban boys in determining their level of home adjustment.
- in the case of rural boys as well as girls, no significant variation seemed to exist between the adolescents of HSFC and the HDFC groups.
- urban boys had better adjustment than their rural counter parts; better home adjustment of adolescents was due to satisfactory family climate.
- in the case of girls, there was no relationship between family climate and home adjustment.

Kaur (1990) stated that males were high on home, health, social and total adjustment.

Aggarwal, S. (1988) found that:

- there was a significant difference between the adjustment problems of more effective and less effective female teachers at primary level, the more effective teachers were better adjusted than their less effective counterparts.
- social factors were found more prominent in the adjustment problems of more effective teachers, while in the case of less effective female teachers the emotional factors were found more influential.

Goyal and Chopra (1989) reported that male SC/ST student teachers had significantly higher self-concept, total adjustment and total achievement than their female SC/ST counterparts.

Sharma (1991) found that most of the boys belonging to SC and ST felt no problem in various fields like academics, family, economic, social, emotional and co-curricular activities and economic adjustment.

Dua (1991) found that working women yielded significantly higher mean values as compared to their non-working counterparts on the variables of emotional adjustment, expectations for social responsibilities, out door work, home management, modern attitudes towards religion, education, family planning, women's status, women's freedom, marriage and caste where as non-working women had obtained higher mean values on the variables of home adjustment, social adjustment, marital adjustment, work expected for children, husband, and for other family members, also on expectations from family members, in comparison to their working counterparts.

Nisha (1991) stated that:

- males high on alienation differed significantly from males low on alienation on neuroticism, lie-scale, aesthetic values, home, emotional and total adjustment as well as self-esteem.
- Females high on alienation differed significantly on psychoticism, extraversion, neuroticism, home, social and total adjustment and self-esteem from female low on alienation.

Chaddam (1985) found that:

- no significant difference was observed between the emotional adjustment scores of various subgroups of teachers, viz., males and females.
- there was a moderate correlation between self concept and emotional adjustment for male teachers.

- there was a moderate correlation between self-concept and emotional adjustment for urban male teachers.
- there was zero or no correlation between scores of self-concept and emotional adjustment for female teachers.

Donga (1987) found that female trainees were more adjusted than male trainees.

Prasad (1985) found that adjustment of teachers was related to their sex and not with the level of their schools; males adjusted better than females.

Tripathi (1981) found that:

- girls were comparatively more adjusted to the home area.
- maladjusted students faced difficulty in maintaining domestic adjustment, economic crisis, educational, environment, etc.; however, girls faced less difficulty in adjusting to these situations.

Nomani, H.R. (1965) found that:

- there was no significant difference in the adjustment of males and females.
- the male and female samples did not significantly differ in different areas of adjustment.
- college boys were superior to the school boys in respect of family adjustment.

Sharma (1979) found that the sex had significant difference on adjustment; the females had higher adjustment scores than the males and also the females had more psychological problems and complexes than the males.

Goswami (1980) reported that the adolescent girls encounter maximum problems in the area of emotional, mental, school study and home adjustment; physical adjustment and sex adjustment were the least problematic for them.

Sujatha (1981) reported that adolescent boys of high income status are better adjusted at home than girls.

Asha (1978) found that:

- the creative groups among the boys showed significant differences in emotional adjustment.
- only two subgroups of boys (high and moderate creative groups) showed significant difference in home adjustment.
- boys and girls differed significantly in adjustment to situations that are assumed to create problems.

Devi (1979) found that:

- there was a significant difference between the adjustment of girls in the experimental and controlled groups in social, health, home, emotional and school areas of adjustment.
- physical education played a very important part in the adjustment of the adolescent girls.

Saun (1980) found that the male high achievers were more adjusted than the low achievers in the area of home and health adjustment.

Kaur (2007) found that:

- women face more marital adjustment problems.
- working women teachers face more marital adjustment problems.
- working women teachers face more marital adjustment problems than non-working women.

Sabu and Jangaiah (2005) found no significant difference between male and female teachers in their adjustment.

Surekha (2008) fount that:

- boys of private schools are better adjusted than boys of government schools.
- girls of private schools are better adjusted than girls of government schools.

Shahpur (2004) reported that boys and girls do not differ in their adjustment.

Vamadevappa (2005) found no significant difference between boys and girls in their adjustment and also in health and educational adjustment areas; where as significant difference was found in their home, social and emotional adjustment; boys have better social and emotional adjustment than girls, but the girls have better home adjustment than boys.

Simons-Morton, et.al. (1999) found that school adjustment was significantly higher among females than males.

2. Adjustment and Locality

Kumari (1990) found that in case of urban and rural juvenile delinquents and adults, rural and urban offenders the total adjustment was significantly correlated with social and emotional adjustment and were significantly related with each other.

Gupta (1990) found that:

- adolescent girls studying in urban schools were significantly better in their social adjustment as compared to girls in rural schools.
- there was +ve (positive) relationship between SES and social adjustment of adolescent girls of private, government, co-educational, girls and English medium schools though this was not found in case of urban, rural and Hindi medium schools.
- parents of girls studying in urban and English medium schools had a better opinion regarding the social adjustment of their daughters as compared to the parents of girls in rural and Hindi medium schools.
- adolescent girls studying in urban, private, co-educational and English-medium schools belonging to the higher SES showed better social adjustment.

Kasinath (1991) found that:

- Hindi and non-Hindi speaking rural students differed significantly in respect of their social adjustment.
- Hindi and non-Hindi speaking rural students did not differ significantly in respect of their emotional and educational adjustment.

- HS rural and NHS urban students did not differ significantly in respect of their total adjustment.

Shah (1989) found that:

- the urban adolescent students form satisfactory family climate had scored significantly higher on home adjustment than their counterparts from dissatisfactory family climate in case of rural adolescents.
- family climate was found to be effective in the case of urban boys, in determining their level of home adjustment.
- in case of rural boys as well as girls, no significant variation seemed to exist between the adolescents of HSFC and the HDFC groups.
- urban boys had better adjustment than their rural counter parts; better home adjustment of adolescents was due to satisfactory family climate.

Kumari (1988) found that sports girls belonging to rural and urban areas were better in emotional, social and educational adjustment than non-sports girls.

Reddy (1974) found that no differences among the subjects from urban, semi-urban and rural localities with regard to scholastic performance as well as academic adjustment.

Chadda (1985) found that:

- no difference was observed between the emotional adjustment scores of various subgroups of teachers, viz., male, female, rural and urban.
- there was a moderate correlation between self-concept and emotional adjustment for urban male teachers.

Babel (1986) found that overall adjustment of Nu (Fiji) was the best that of Uganda and Zaire the worst.

Lal (1985) found that there was a statistically significant difference between the rural SC group of subjects and the rural general category group of subjects on the adjustment.

Nomani (1965) found that:

- no significant difference was found in the adjustment of Ranchi and Simdega samples.
- a significant difference was found in health adjustments of Ranchi and Simdega samples.
- Ranchi school students tended to have better health adjustment than Simdega school students; but the difference was statistically not significant.

Kamalesh (1981) found that:

- the level of adjustment among the urban SC students belonging to lower socio-economic status was below normal.
- the non-SC students, both of urban and rural areas, did not have adjustment problems.

Sharma (1979) found that the urban students had higher adjustment scores on VPP than the rural students where as the urban students had higher maladjustment scores on ISB.

Karbassi (1981) found that:

- Iranian students who were jobless in Iran showed poor social adjustment.
- educational aspirations of only young Iranian students varied with social adjustment.

Pandey (1979) found that among students of higher secondary stage, the rural group to be better in emotional, health and school adjustment where as the urban group is better in aesthetic adjustment' significant relationship exists among adjustment aspiration and achievement.

Saun (1980) found that:

- the urban low achievers were emotionally more adjusted than high achievers but they were equally adjusted in the remaining areas of A.I.
- the rural high and low achievers differed significantly in their level of adjustment in three areas, namely, home, social and educational.

3. Adjustment and Age

Jamuna (1985) found that middle aged and older women differed significantly in their level of adjustment.

Goyal and Chopra (1989) found that, SC/ST student teachers upto 25 years of age were found to be having higher total self concept and achievement than those in the age group of 25 years and above. However, the groups did not differ on adjustment.

Nisha (1991) found that adolescents of 13 to 14 years of age were high on alienation on extraversion, home, social, emotional and total adjustment, self esteem and locus of control.

Donga (1987) found that no significant effect of marital status, level of education, status in family and age on adjustment. There was no significant effect of interaction between age, marital status and educational qualification upon adjustment.

Subrahmanian (1989) stated that elderly males and females differed significantly in perception of support, adjustment, role activity, involvement and satisfaction.

Sabu and Jangaiah (2005) found that no significant difference among the teachers of different age groups with regard to their adjustment.

4. Adjustment and Experience

Donga (1987) found that:

- the group having teaching experience of two years was more maladjusted than the other.
- the trainees having teaching experience in primary schools were highly adjusted.
- there was no significant effect of interaction between faculty, teaching experience and sex upon adjustment.

Sabu and Jangaiah (2005) found a significant difference among the teachers with varying length of experience in their adjustment.

5. Adjustment and Management

Surekha (2008) found that:

- the students of private schools were better adjusted than students of government schools.
- boys of private schools were better adjusted than boys of government schools.
- girls of private schools were better adjusted than girls of government schools.
- the students of private schools were better than students of government schools.

Gaur (1988) found that:

- the teacher educators of the unaided training colleges faced many problems.
- the teacher educators of autonomous institutions of Rajasthan faced problems.

Gupta (1990) found that adolescent girls studying in private schools showed significantly better social adjustment as compared to those of government schools.

6. Adjustment and Family Climate

Shah (1991) found that students from an unsatisfactory family climate showed better adjustment in schools than students from a satisfactory family climate.

Shah (1989) found that:

- the home adjustment of students having satisfactory family climate was found to be far superior to that of those who had highly dissatisfactory family climate.
- in case of girls, family climate did not play an important role in determining the level of home adjustment.
- in case of urban students, the adolescents from satisfactory family climate had scored significantly higher on home adjustment than their counterparts from dissatisfactory family climate in case of rural adolescent.

- family climate was found to be effective in case of urban boys in determining their level of home adjustment.
- in case of the entire group of adolescents, significant and positive relationship was observed between family climate and home adjustment.
- in case of girls, there was no relationship between family climate and home adjustment.

7. Adjustment and Teachers

Gupta (1988) found that:

- science and arts teachers did not differ significantly with respect to adjustment and academic and general environment of institution.
- effective arts teachers were significantly better adjusted socially, psychologically and physically than effective science teachers.
- effective arts teachers were found significantly better adjusted in personal life than effective science teachers.
- effective arts teachers were significantly higher than effective science teachers on financial adjustment and job satisfaction.
- effective arts teachers were significantly superior to effective science teachers with regard to total adjustment.

Aggarwal (1988) found that:

- there was a significant difference between the adjustment problems of more effective and less effective female teachers at primary level.
- the more effective teachers were better adjusted than their effective counterparts.
- social factors were found to be more prominent in the adjustment problems of more effective teachers while in case of less effective female teachers the emotional factors were found to be more influential.

Prasad (1985) found that

- adjustment of teachers was related to their sex and not with the level of their schools.
- primary and secondary teachers were almost similar in their total adjustment.

Sabu and Jangaiah (2005) found that:

- there was no significant difference between male and female teachers in their adjustment.
- there was no significant difference among the teachers with number of inservice programs attended with regard to their adjustment.
- there is a significant difference among the teachers with varying lengths of experience in their adjustment.
- there is no significant difference among the teachers with different qualifications in their adjustment.

8. Adjustment and Self-concept

Vijaya Laxmi (1991) found that the self concept of the children was related to their personality adjustment.

Goyal and Chopra (1989) found that:

- there was no significant difference in the total adjustment and self concept of SC/ST and non SC/ST student teachers.
- non-SC/ST student teachers exhibited higher self-concept, had better social adjustment and higher achievement in theory and practice teaching than their SC/ST counterparts.
- male SC/ST student teachers had a significantly higher total self concept, total adjustment and total achievement than their SC/ST counter parts.
- no significant relationship was found between self-concept, adjustment and attitude with the achievement of female SC/ST student teachers.

- home adjustment, educational adjustment, social adjustment, emotional adjustment and self concept about abilities predicted the achievement of SC/ST student teachers to a significant level.

Chadda (1985) found that there was zero or no correlation between scores of self concept and emotional adjustment of female teachers.

9. Adjustment and Socio-economic Status

Grewal (1986) found that:

- the subjects of 3 socio-economic levels, i.e., high, middle and low differed on the variables of physical fitness, attitude towards physical activity and adjustment.
- the middle socio-economic group was better adjusted to the variables of adjustment over the low socio-economic group; there was a significant difference between home adjustment of middle socio-economic group and high socio-economic group; but there was no significant difference in home adjustment of high SES group and low SES group.
- all the socio-economic groups showed that there was no relationship between physical fitness and adjustment.

Tripati (1981) found that adjusted students had comparatively better socio-economic background.

Kamalesh (1981) found that the level of adjustment among urban S.C. students belonging to lower socio-economic status was below normal.

Sharma (1979) found that the socio-economic status had no effect on adjustment.

10. Adjustment and Spoken Language

Kasinath (1991) found that:

- Hindi and non-Hindi speaking boys did not differ significantly in respect of their emotional and educational adjustment.
- Hindi and non-Hindi speaking boys differ significantly in respect of their social adjustment.

- HS and NHS girls did not differ significantly in respect of their emotional, social and educational adjustment.
- HS and NHS rural students did not differ significantly in respect of their emotional and educational adjustment.
- HS and NHS rural students differed significantly in respect of their social adjustment.
- HS boys and NHS girls did not differ significantly in respect of their total adjustment.
- HS girls and NHS boys did not differ significantly in respect of their total adjustment.
- HS rural and NHS urban students did not differ significantly in respect of their total adjustment.

11. Adjustment and Medium

Gupta (1990) found that:

- adolescent girls studying in English medium schools were significantly better in their social adjustment as compared to girls of Hindi medium schools.
- parents of girls studying in urban and English medium schools had a better opinion regarding the social adjustment of their daughters as compared to the parents of girls in rural and Hindi medium schools.
- adolescent girls studying in urban, private, co-educational and English medium schools belonging to the higher SES showed better social adjustment.

12. Adjustment and Achievers

Saun (1980) found that:

- the male high achievers were more adjusted than the low achievers in the areas of home and health adjustment.
- significant difference existed between the high and the low achieving females in health, social, emotional and educational areas of adjustment.
- the urban low achievers were emotionally more adjusted than the high achievers, but they were equally adjusted in the remaining areas of A.I.

- the rural high and low achievers differed significantly in their level of adjustment in 3 areas, namely, home, social and educational.
- high and low achieving adolescents had shown different adjustment patterns in home, social and educational areas.

Prasanna (1984) found that high and low achievers have differential adjustment patterns.

13. Adjustment and Effectiveness

Gupta (1988) found that:

- effective arts teachers were significantly better adjusted socially, psychologically and physically than effective science teachers.
- effective arts teachers were found significantly better adjusted in personal life that effective science teachers.
- effective arts teachers were significantly higher than effective science teaches on financial adjustment and job satisfaction.

Aggarwal (1988) found that:

- there was a significant difference between the adjustment problems of more effective and less effective female teachers at primary level. The more effective teachers were better adjusted than their less effective counterparts.
- social factors were found more prominent in the adjustment a problems of more effective teacher while in the case of less effective female teachers the emotional factors were found more influential.

14. Adjustment and Economic Condition

Sujatha Rani (1981) reported that adolescent boys of high income status are better adjusted at home than girls.

Subrahmanian (1989) found that demographic factors such as income, education and marital status influenced perception of support, dimensions of adjustments.

Donga (1987) found that:

- the middle income group was most maladjusted.
- there was no significant effect of interaction between income, residential accommodation and social status upon adjustment.

Tulpule (1977) found that:

- the lower middle income group was the most maladjusted group in the area of home adjustment.
- in emotional adjustment, both the lower and higher income groups were more maladjusted.
- the higher income group was superior to other groups without a single case of maladjustment.

15. Adjustment and Scheduled Castes

Lal (1985) found that:

- there was a positive and significant relationship between general life adjustment and personality.
- there was a significant positive relationship between intelligence and home adjustment for the scheduled caste sample.
- there was a significant difference between the rural SC group of subjects and the rural general category group of subjects on adjustment.

Kamalesh (1981) found that:

- the level of adjustment among the urban SC students belonging to lower socio-economic status was below normal.
- the non-SC students, both in urban and rural areas did not have adjustment problems.

16. Adjustment and Scheduled Tribes

Chobey (1990) found that:

- no difference was found in the academic adjustment of socially high and socially low deprived tribal youths.

- there was no significant relationship between the scores obtained on the academic adjustment inventory and social deprivation scale in the case of socially high and low deprived tribal youth.
- no relationship was found between the academic adjustment and scholastic adjustment of socially high and socially low deprived tribal youth.

Kuman (1989) found that:

- there existed no difference in adjustment between tribals and non-tribals.
- adjustment and attitude towards school were found to be associated positively and significantly both in case of tribal as well as non-tribal students.
- level of aspiration was found to be related to attitude towards school, adjustment and educational interest either for tribal or non-tribal students.

17. Adjustment and Scheduled Castes and Scheduled Tribes.

Sujatha and Yeshodhara (1986) found that:

- SC and ST students had relatively poor school adjustment compared to non- SC/ST students.
- a significant association between the academic achievement and school adjustment was found in case of SC/ST students but not in case of non SC/ST students.

Goyal and Chopra (1989) found that:

- there was no significant difference in the total adjustment and self-concept of SC/ST and non-SC/ST student teachers.
- Non SC/ST student teachers exhibited higher self-concept had better social adjustment and higher achievement in theory and practical teaching than their SC/ST counterparts.

- male SC/ST students teachers had a significantly higher total self concept, total adjustment and total achievement than their female SC/ST counterparts.
- SC/ST student teachers upto 25 years of age were found to be having a higher total self concept and achievement than those in the group of 25 years and above.
- no significant relationship was found between self-concept, adjustment and attitude with achievement of female SC/ST student teachers.
- home adjustment, educational adjustment, social adjustment, emotional adjustment and self-concept about abilities could used to predicted the achievement of SC/ST student teachers to a significant level.
- worthiness, emotional maturity and emotional adjustment seemed to predict the achievement of non SC/ST student teachers to a significant level.
- achievement of all student teachers could be predicted through their home adjustment, worthiness and educational adjustment.

Sharma (1991) found that most of the boys belonging to SC and ST felt no problem in various fields like academics, family, economic, social, emotional and co-curricular activities and economic adjustment.

18. Adjustment and Researchers

Kaur (1990) found that:

- science researchers were found to highest on theoretical and economic values; arts researchers scored highest on social, emotional and total adjustment.
- professional researchers scored highest on home and health adjustment.
- males were high on home, health, social, emotional and total adjustment.
- scholarship holders were found to be highest on home, health, social, emotional, total adjustment.

19. Adjustment and Physically Handicapped

Banerjee (1988) found that:

- the distribution of the two groups, VH and VN according to the intensity of total adjustment was found to be significant.
- the group of VH adolescents varied with age of onset of the handicap in their adjustment to the interacting environment.

Singh and Chudasama (1992) found that:

- the normal students of standards VIII and IX were better adjusted than physically handicapped students of standards VIII and IX respectively.
- among the physically handicapped students, Hindu and Muslim students were better adjusted as compared to Jain students.

Williams (1981) found that:

- both the blind and deaf children had a good level of home adjustment.
- both the blind and deaf children had a low level of adjustment with their teachers.
- the blind children of classes V, VI and VII were better adjusted in schools than the deaf children; the level of school adjustment of the blind and the deaf was found to decrease as they moved from class V to VII.
- the blind showed better adjusted than the deaf in all the standards in the area of general adjustment.
- in all areas taken together, the blind showed better adjustment than the deaf.

Singh (1982) found that:

- there was a difference in general adjustment ability of mentally gifted and retarded students.
- adjustment problems of mentally retarded students were different.

20. Adjustment and Sports

Kumari (1988) found that sports girls belonging to rural and urban areas were better in emotional, social and educational adjustment than non-sports girls.

Devi (1979) found that physical education played a very important part in the adjustment of the adolescent girls.

21. Adjustment in Drug Addicts

Sharma, Hindang Mayun Ibomcha (1990) found that drug addicts were poor in all areas of adjustment except social adjustment.

Gowtham (1992) found that drug users had lack of adjustment.

22. Adjustment and Religion

Sinh and Chudasama (1992) found that Hindu and Muslim students were better adjusted as compared to Jain students among the physically handicapped students.

Shirotriya (1988) found that:

- no difference in marital adjustment among Hindu and Christian males and females, but a significant difference was found between Muslim males and females.
- SES was significantly related to marital adjustment.
- males and females differed in marital adjustment on the basis of religiousity.

23. Adjustment and Alienation

Nisha (1991) found that:

- adolescents high on alienation differed significantly from those who were low on alienation on the scores of all the dimensions of personality, aesthetic values, home, social, emotional and total adjustment and self-esteem.
- males high on alienation differed significantly from males low on alienation on neuroticism, lie-scale, aesthetic values, home, emotional and total adjustment as well as self-esteem.

- females high on alienation differed significantly on psychoticism, extraversion, neuroticism, home, social and total adjustment and self-esteem from females low on alienation.

24. Adjustment and Creative Students

Setia (1989) stated that:

- high and low creative students of all the faculties did not differ significantly regarding the different dimensions of adjustment, except for the health adjustment scores of high and low creative students of the family of commerce.
- the high creative students of different faculties did not differ among themselves in respect of different dimensions of adjustment, except in case of emotional adjustment scores of science and art faculties.
- low creative students of different faculties differ significantly regarding scores on various dimensions of adjustment.

Asha (1978) found that:

- none of the groups classified on the basis of creativity showed significant difference in health, social and school adjustment areas for the boys and girls.
- the three creative groups among the boys showed significant differences in emotional adjustment.
- only two subgroups (high and moderate creative groups) of boys showed significant difference in home adjustment.
- boys and girls differed significantly in adjustment to situations that are assumed to create problems for creative children.
- the better adjusted and maladjusted groups with in each area of adjustment differed only in certain tasks of creativity and these tasks differed for each area of adjustment.

25. Adjustment and Administrative Effectiveness

Aggarwal (1983) stated that:

- adjustment of principals was found to be a powerful predictor of their administrative effectiveness.
- adjustment of principals to the teachers was not found to be significantly related to their administrative effectiveness.
- adjustment of principals to students was highly related to their administrative effectiveness; a similar results was found in the case of principals' adjustment to ministerial staff.
- adjustment of principals to management was not found to be related to their administrative effectiveness.
- adjustment of principals to higher authorities was not found to be a significant factor of administrative effectiveness.
- adjustment of principals to community was not found to be a significant predictor of their administrative effectiveness.
- principals' stress proneness, adjustment and job satisfaction combined together were found to be significant predictors of their administrative effectiveness.
- the adjustment of principals and their job satisfaction was found to be mutually related to their administrative effectiveness.

26. Adjustment and Offenders

Kumari (1990) found that:

- offenders were maladjusted in all the areas of adjustment.
- in case of urban and rural juvenile delinquents and adult rural and urban offenders, total adjustment was significantly correlated with social and emotional adjustment and were significantly related with each other.

- in case of juvenile and adult female offenders, no significant differences were observed in case of personality characteristics, intelligence, achievement motivation and adjustment, except in case of SES and health adjustment.

27. Adjustment and Streams

Mulia (1990) stated that:

- there was no significant difference in leadership behaviour among the three streams, viz., commerce, arts and science as well as among different levels of adjustment.
- there was no significant interaction effect of streams and adjustment.
- there was no significant interaction effect of streams, sex and adjustment.

28. Adjustment and Discordance

Sharma and Mehta (1989) found that:

- subjects having psychological discordance between chosen curriculum, i.e., science and scientific interest were found to have significantly lower psychological adjustment in comparison to subjects having concordance; there was a significant effect not only on the total adjustment but also on the separate areas of emotional and educational adjustment.
- there was no effect of discordance between chosen curriculum and scientific aptitude upon psychological adjustment.
- there was no effect of discordance between scientific interest and scientific aptitude upon psychological adjustment.

29. Adjustment and Orphan

Swami (1989) stated that:

- Normal students were better adjusted than orphan students.

- Sex, grade and religion had no effect on the difference in adjustment of orphan and normal students

30. Adjustment and Adolescents

Dabas (1984) stated that school segregation produced historical and psycho-social adjustment among adolescent girls.

Sunitha (1986) found that the absence of a sound study procedure raises doubts concerning the validity of generalization that motor proficiency in relation to maladjustment processes of school and college students.

Srivastava (1981) stated that most of the experiments on adjustments indicate that an increase in the level of adjustment of adolescents led to positive self-esteem, where as deterioration in adjustment led to negative self-esteem.

Gupta, Sushma (1990) found that:

- adolescent girls studying in urban schools were significantly better in their social adjustment as compared to girls in rural students.
- adolescent girls studying in private schools showed significantly better social adjustment as compared to those of government schools.
- adolescent girls studying in co-educational schools were significantly better in their social adjustment as compared to adolescents of girl's schools.
- adolescent girls studying in English medium schools were significantly better in their social adjustment as compared to girls of Hindi medium schools.
- education of father and education of mother positively influenced in social adjustment of adolescent girls.
- adolescent girls studying in urban, private, co-educational and English medium schools belonging to the higher SES showed better social adjustment.

Sharma (1990) stated that drug addicted adolescents were poor in all areas of adjustment except social adjustment.

Shah (1989) found that:

- in case of urban students, the adolescents from satisfactory family climate had scored significantly higher on home adjustment than their counterparts from dissatisfactory family climate in case of rural adolescents.
- in case of rural boys as well as girls, no significant variation seemed to exist between the adolescents of HSFC and the HDFC groups.
- in case of the entire group of adolescents, significant and positive relationship was observed between family climate and home adjustment.
- urban boys had better adjustment than their rural counterparts; better home adjustment of adolescents was due to satisfactory family climate.
- in case of girls, there was no relationship between family climate and home adjustment.

Nisha (1991) stated that:

- adolescents high on alienation differed significantly from those who were low on alienation on the scores of all the dimensions of personality, aesthetic values, home, social, emotional and total adjustment and self-esteem.
- adolescents of 13 to 14 years of age high on alienation on extraversion, home, social, emotional and total adjustment, self-esteem and locus of control.

Devi (1979) found that physical education played a very important part in the adjustment of the adolescent girls.

Sawn (1980) stated that high and low achieving adolescents had shown different adjustment patterns in home, social and emotional areas.

31. Adjustment and Scholastic Abilities

Mehta et.al. (1988) found that:

- boys with superior scholastic ability (SSA) differed from boys with average scholastic ability (ASA) with regard to sensitivity to problems relating to finance and living conditions, adjustment to school curriculum and teaching procedure, family and sex.

- basically, there was not much difference in adjustment problems between the two groups.

32. Adjustment and Intellectual Commitment

Srivastava (1989) stated that:

- the need system of students contributed to the prediction of intellectual commitment and college adjustment.
- the positive and satisfying experience of group atmosphere and the college environment; complementing student needs was found to be related to high intellectual commitment and good college adjustment.
- the correlation analysis confirmed the null hypothesis of no relationship among family interaction, intellectual commitment and college adjustment of students.
- the null hypothesis of no relationship among teacher style and intellectual commitment and college adjustment of students did not find support in the personal study.

33. Adjustment and Parents Education

Gupta (1990) stated that:

- education of father and education of mother positively influenced the social adjustment of adolescent girls.
- parents of girls studying in urban and English medium schools had a better opinion regarding the social adjustment of their daughter's as compared to the parents of girls in rural and Hindi medium schools.
- parents of girls studying in urban and English medium schools had a better opinion regarding the social adjustment of their daughter's as compared to the parents of girls in rural and Hindi medium schools.

34. Adjustment and Children of Working and Non-Working Mothers

Gaikarad (1988) found that the well adjusted mothers were found using healthy child rearing practices but the correlation coefficients failed to bring out any significant relationship.

Jain (1990) found that a significant difference in academic achievement in case of children of working uneducated (WUE), working educated (WE), non-working uneducated (NWUE), non-working educated (NWE), and WE-NWE having high adjustment; total (T), emotional (E), social (S) and educational (Ed) adjustments except in case of WE-NWE children having high E adjustment; NWUE-NWE children having high S adjustment.

Chhaganlal (1992) stated that:

- teachers children were with better adjustment than non-teachers children.
- primary, secondary and college teachers children did not differ significantly in adjustment.

35. Adjustment and Frustration

Goyal (1988) stated that, interaction between different areas of adjustment and different modes of frustration was significant, except in case of aggression and emotional adjustment.

Gupta (1990) found significant negative correlation between frustration and (a) adjustment (b) intelligence and (c) academic achievement.

36. Adjustment and Intelligence

Tripathi (1981) stated that intelligence and adjustment were mutually dependent.

Lal (1985) found that:

- there was a significant positive relationship between intelligence and the home adjustment area for the scheduled caste sample.
- there was no relationship between intelligence and adjustment areas except financial adjustment for the general category sample.

37. Adjustment and Sociometric Status

Rather (1990) found that:

- socio-metric status was positively and significantly related to adjustment.
- girls were found socially better adjusted than boys.

Pathak (1971) reported that socio-metric status was significantly related to various way of adjustment.

38. Adjustment and Achievement

Mathur (1963), Kumar (1964), Srivastava (1967) stated that adjustment problems have been found to be negatively associated with achievement.

Ramachandran (1990), Ray, P. (1990), Baskaran, K. (1990), Diwan, O.K. (1991), Vamadevappa, H.V. (2000), Rao, S.N. (1963), Singh (1965), Abraham, M. (1974), H.S. Kaile and Kaur (1995) found that academic achievement was positively related to adjustment.

Srivastava (1967), Sharma (1972), Dhaliwal (1971), Chaudari Jain (1975), Nagapal, R. (1979), Premalata Sharma (1981), Shahpur (1994) reported that under achievers have poorer adjustment when compared to over achievers.

Bhatt (1971) reported that under achievers showed better level of adjustment than the over achievers.

Siva Prasadh (2005) found a significant and positive relationship between adjustment and achievement of students belonging to A.P. residential schools.

Roy (1969) found that the low achievers have poorer overall adjustment compared with the high achievers.

Pandey (1979) found a significant relationship between adjustment and achievement.

Mehrotra (1986) found a positive relationship between level of adjustment and academic achievement.

39. Adjustment and Teacher Educators

Goyal (1980) found that:

- a large majority of the teacher educators were favourably inclined towards their profession and were satisfied in the job. However, they were not well adjusted and had low professional interest.

- attitude, job satisfaction and occupational adjustment among teacher educators were associated with one another, where as social and emotional adjustment and professional interests were not related with other variables.

Gaur (1985) found that:

- the teachers educators of the unaided training colleges faced many problems.
- the teacher educators of unaided training colleges of Rajasthan did not get the UGC grade; they did not get any educational and vocational opportunities; they work hard under the pressure of the management committee and face other problems related to recreation, religion, etc.
- the teacher educators of the correspondence department of Rajastan University, Jaipur faced many problems.
- the teacher educators of the autonomous institutions of Rajastan faced problems like insecurity of job, a prescribed dress for the teacher, excessive work load and other problems relating to religion, region, etc.
- there was a significant difference between the problems of teacher educators of different training colleges.
- there was no significant difference among the problems of male and female groups.

Most of the studies quoted are mainly concerned to the groups other than the targeted one. Even then, all the studies related to adjustment were cited in order to make the readers aware of the studies undertaken in the area of adjustment. Hence, the present study has been considered for research and analysis.

3

Research Methodology

"Research design is the arrangement of conditions for collection and analysis of data in a manner that aims to combine relevance to the research purpose with economy in procedure."

—Claires Clitz

METHOD OF RESEARCH

Research is considered to be the more formal, systematic, and intensive process of carrying on the scientific method of analysis. It involves a more systematic structure of investigation usually resulting in conclusions. (J.W. Best)

Research is an endless quest for knowledge and an unending search for truth. It brings to light the new knowledge or correct the previous errors and misconceptions and adds new things in an orderly way to the existing body of knowledge. The knowledge obtained by research is scientific and objective and is a matter of rational understanding, common verification and experience.

Research is an honest, exhaustive, intelligent searching for facts and their meanings or implications with reference to a given problem. It is the process of arriving at dependable solutions to a problem through planned and systematic collection, analysis and interpretation of data. The best research is that which is reliable, verifiable and exhaustive so that it provides information in which we have confidence (P.M. Cook).

The formidable problem that follows the test of defining the research problem is the preparation of the design of the research project, popularly known as the research design. Decision regarding what, where, when, how much and by what means concerning an inquiring or research study constitute a research design.

A research design is the arrangement of conditions for collection and analysis of data in a manner that aims to combine relevance to the research purpose with the economics of the procedure.

In fact, the research design is the conceptual structure within which research is conducted. It constitutes the blue print for the collection, measurement and analysis of data. As such, the design includes an outline of what the researcher will do from writing the hypothesis and its operational implications to the final analysis of data.

Research design is needed because it facilitates the smooth sailing of various research operations, there by making research as efficient as possible yielding maximum information with minimal expenditure of effort, time and money.

A good design is often characterized by objectives like flexibility, appropriateness, efficiency, economy and so on. Generally the design which minimizes bias and maximizes the reliability of the data collected and analysed is considered a good design. The design which gives the smallest experimental error is supposed to be the best design in many investigations. Similarly, a design that fields maximal information and provides an opportunity for considering many different aspects of a problem is considered most appropriate and efficient design in respect of many research problems. Thus the question of good design is related to the purpose or objective of the research problem and also which the nature of the problem to be studied. A design may be quite suitable in one case, but may be found waste in one respect or the other in the context of some other research problem.

Design is the heart of any research. Research design is a plan which enables one to reason logically sound conclusions from observed facts. It involves the arrangement of conditions and observations in such a way that alternative answers to the questions take up in research are ruled out. It contains built in systems of checks against all factors that might affect the validity of the research outcome. These two basic purposes of design of are to provide a conclusive answers to the problem posed by the research and to control the potentially relevant variables that are those which may also influence the research outcome, but in which the researcher is not interested at the movement. (D. Bhaskara Rao)

The descriptive or normative survey method of educational research is very common in most of the educational studies. It is that method of investigation which attempts to describe and interpret what exists at present in the form of conditions practices, processes, trends, effects, attitudes, beliefs, etc. It is concerned with the phenomena that are typical of the normal conditions. It investigates into the conditions or relationships that exist in practice and that prevail; beliefs, points of view or attitudes that are held; processes that are influencing, that are being felt and trends that are developing. It is an organized attempt to analyze, interpret and report the present status of a social institution, group or area.

OPERATIONAL DEFINITIONS OF KEY TERMS

The operational definitions of the important terms used in the present study on "A Study of Adjustment of Teacher Educators" are discussed and defined here with.

1. Study

Study refers to a systematic investigation which is objective and research-oriented.

2. Teacher Educators

Teacher educators are the higher education faculty responsible for teacher preparation.

3. Adjustment

Adjustment is a process by which behavioural changes produce harmonious relationship between him and the environment.

4. Gender

Gender refers to male and female teacher educators.

5. Locality

Locality refers to rural and urban. Urban Teacher Educators are those who are working in the Colleges of Education located in urban areas. Rural Teacher Educators are those who are working in the Colleges of Education located in rural areas.

6. Management

Management refers to aided and unaided Colleges of Education. Aided Colleges are those which get financial assistance from the government. Unaided Colleges are those which do not get any financial support from the government.

7. Experience

Experience refers to above 15 years or below 15 years working in any institution as teacher educators.

8. Age

Age refers to above 45 years and below 45 years of teacher educators.

VARIABLES OF THE STUDY

Variables are the conditions or characteristics that the experimenter manipulates, controls or observes. There are mainly three types of variables, namely, independent, dependent and intervening. The independent variables are those variables which do not change on manipulation by the experimenter. The dependent variables are those variables which change on manipulation done by the experimenter. The intervening variables are those variables which are dependant both on dependent and independent variables.

For the present study, the following independent variables are chosen:

1. Gender

Men and Women Teacher Educators

2. Locality

Rural and Urban Teacher Educators

3. Management

Aided and Unaided Colleges of Education.

4. Experience

Teaching Experience with above and below 15 years of Teacher Educators.

5. Age

Teacher Educators aged above 45 years and below 45 years.

It was found in the previous studies that there existed and not existed a significant difference in the adjustment of male and female, rural and urban, aided and unaided, more experience and less experienced and higher aged and lesser aged teachers. So, to know if any difference exists in this study also, the above variables were considered.

HYPOTHESES OF THE STUDY

Hypothesis is a tentative generalization which provides basis to the whole study to be tested by facts. It is a shrewd and intelligent guess, supposition, inference, hunch, provisional statement, a tentative generalization to the existence of some fact, condition or relationship relative to some phenomenon which serves to explain already known facts in a given area of knowledge and which guides the search for new truth on the basis of empirical evidence.

In statistical hypothesis, the sample should be representative of the whole population. This can be ensured in stratified random sampling where the units of population have got equal chances of being represented. The hypothesis to be tested in this study is 'Null Hypothesis'. Ordinarily, a null hypothesis is a statement to believe that there is no relation between or among variables. Once it is formulated, depending on the outcome, it will be either accepted or rejected. For the present study keeping the objectives in view, the following hypotheses were formulated.

Hypothesis 1

Teacher educators are not having high adjustment.

Hypothesis 2

There is no significant difference between the adjustment of men and women teacher educators.

Hypothesis 3

There is no significant difference between the adjustment of rural and urban teacher educators.

Hypothesis 4

There is no significant difference between the adjustment of aided and unaided teacher educators.

Hypothesis 5

There is no significant difference between the adjustment of teacher educators having experience below 15 years and above 15 years.

Hypothesis 6

There is no significant difference between the adjustment of teacher educators aged below 45 years and above 45 years.

SAMPLE OF THE STUDY

After finalizing the variables of the present study consideration was given to whether the entire population is to be made the subject for data collection or a particular group is to be selected as representative of the whole population. The entire population here refers to all the teacher educators of Krishna, Guntur and Srikakulam districts.

Of the above two techniques, the selection of a group as a representative of the whole population was found to be more convenient and suitable. This technique leads to considerable saving of time, effort and finance. The number of teacher educators selected will be small, and so it is possible to make a detailed and intensive study. This generally leads to more accurate and reliable results. As this sampling technique has many advantages, it was selected for the collection of data.

In any social research, various methods are utilized for selection and drawing of samples. After a detailed study of all these methods and considering the variables selected for the research work, the stratified sampling method areas found to be most suitable.

In the stratified sampling method, the entire population is divided into smaller homogeneous groups or strata and then a sample is selected within each group. Every sampling unit in the population is placed in one of the strata prior to the selection of the sample so that the sum of the strata is identical with the population.

Stratified sampling method has certain merits and advantages as a technique of sampling. Auckoff has rightly said that stratified sampling enables the researcher to make a comparison of properties of the strata as well as to estimate the population characteristics.

In this stratified sampling method, the investigator has greater control over the selection of the sample when compared with random sampling. In random sampling, although every group has a chance of being selected and included in the sample, there is every possibility and some times it does happen that certain important groups are left unrepresented. But, in stratified sampling method, no important group is likely to be left out.

Stratified sampling method is the ideal one when comparison between different variables has to be made. For example, if comparison has to be made between teacher educators of aided and unaided colleges or rural and urban teacher educators, it would be very difficult to select the required member of units through any other method of sampling. If any other method is used, the problem of bias and prejudice creeps in.

Replacement of units is also possible in the stratified sampling method. Normally, if a particular unit is not assessable for the study, it is difficult to replace it by another, but in this method it is possible. Stephen states that stratification automatically brings about a replacement of persons lost to the sample by persons of the same stratum, thus partly correcting the bias that would result if there were no replacement of loses.

In stratified sampling method, much depends on stratification process. The following precautions were taken while stratifying the population. The variables involved in the study were taken note of, care was taken to see that each stratum in the universe was large enough in size so that each stratum of items could be done on random bias, the strata formed were definite and clear cut, each stratum was free from influence of the other and that there was no overlapping.

Before actually selecting the sample, certain fundamental principles were also considered to make the sample scientific and clear cut.

Firstly, the universe was clearly defined. In the technical phraseology of research, the whole population out of which the samples are selected is known as the universe. For the present research work, the universe includes all the teacher educators of Colleges of Education of Andhra Pradesh. The study was limited to particular geographical areas, viz., Krishna, Guntur and Srikakulam districts, to facilitate appropriate sample selection and to avoid bias and prejudice.

According to the second principle, decision has to be made about the unit of the sample. A unit of sample may be a house, a family, a group of individuals or a single individual. A good unit should possess these characteristics: 1. *Clarity:* The unit should be clearly defined in unambiguous terms. This would make the study easy and efficient. For the present research work, a sampling unit is defined as a teacher educator of Krishna, Guntur and Srikakulam districts; 2. *Suitability:* A good unit should be well suited to the problem under study. Since the problem is on the identification of level of adjustment of teacher educators, the unit selected is well suited to the problem; 3. *Accessibility:* The unit selected should be easily accessible to the researcher. If the units selected are difficult to reach and if he fails to make use of them the study would be vitiated. The selected sampling unit, i.e., a teacher educator is easily accessible since he/she could be approached in any College of Education.

The third principle to be considered while selecting a sample is the availability and preparation of the source list. There is an important factor that makes representative selection possible. A source list is the list from which the sample may be selected. It may exist even before the beginning of the project or it may be prepared afresh by the investigator himself. Without a source list, study through the sampling method is not possible. For the present research work a source list consisting of the names of Colleges of Education in Krishna, Guntur and Srikakulam districts prepared by the National Council for Teacher Education is used. This source list was found to be relevant and suitable because it included College of Education as the study deals with the teacher educators.

Besides considering these principles it is extremely important to think about the size of the sample to be selected. If the sample is either too small or too large, it will make the study difficult and also makes the results untenable. According to Parten, an optimum sample in a survey is one which fulfills the requirements of effective representativeness, reliability and flexibility. The sample should be small enough to avoid intolerable sampling error. The size of the sample for the present research work was decided after considering the following factors.

(a) Since a detailed study was planned a very large number of sample was not selected. In case of an intensive study, a very large number of samples is not so useful as it involves huge consumption of resources. A smaller sample was found to be convenient.

(b) The size and selection of the sample will also be influenced by the nature of the universe. If the universe is homogeneous, even a small sized sample may yield dependable and required results. If the universe is heterogeneous, small-sized samples will not be useful. In case of present study, the heterogeneous universe was split into smaller homogeneous strata (groups) and the samples were selected from these strata. For example, all the teacher educators of Krishna, Guntur and Srikakulam districts were broadly grouped under male and female. A sample was selected from each of these two groups.

(c) The researcher needs to determine the number of the groups to be formed. In case the number of groups proposed is large, size of the samples shall have to be large so that every group should be of proper size and suit to the requirements of the study. In case the number of groups proposed is small even small-sized samples can be fulfill the requirement. In case of the present study, practical considerations like the availability of resources and time were taken into consideration. Care was taken to make the sample selection technique as scientific as possible.

(d) The size of the sample is also governed by the size of the tools to be used. In case the tools are short and the questions used pertain to certain limited factors, a large sample can be selected. In case the tools are large and the questions are complicated, the sample should be small in size so that from administrative point of view the researcher may not put to unnecessary trouble. In the present study, the tool selected was quite elaborate and makes think carefully to attend to it, hence a very large sample was not selected.

(e) The sampling method also determines the size of the sample. When random sampling method is used the samples have to be large. On the other hand, if samples are selected through stratified sampling method the reliability can be achieved even with the help of the small-sized samples.

Taking into consideration all these factors which influence the size of the sample it was decided that an ideal sample would consist of one hundred and thirty teacher educators. This sample is small enough to avoid unnecessary expenditure and large enough to avoid intolerable sampling error.

After deciding about the sampling method and the size of the sample, the universe selected was divided into different strata. The variables chosen for the study were considered to divide the universe. The variables chosen were male versus female, rural versus urban, aided versus unaided teacher educators, experience, and age.

The stratified random sampling method was selected for the present study. Stratified random sampling is applied as this method of selection assures each individual unit in the universe an equal chance of being chosen. This is suitable for the present study as the universe considered for the study is homogeneous.

The sample consisted of 130 teacher educators working in the Colleges of Education of Guntur, Prakasam and Srikakulam districts.

TOOL OF THE STUDY

A research tool is a tool which has reliability and validity. It is used for the purpose of data collection. Reliability is the degree of consistency that the instrument or procedure demonstrates. Validity is that quality of a data gathering instrument or procedure which enables it to measure what it is supposed to measure.

A research tool plays a major role in any worthwhile research, as it is the sole factor in determining sound data and in arriving at perfect conclusions about the problem or study in hand, which ultimately helps in providing suitable remedial measures to the problem concerned. The selection and use of tool can be done in two ways. The first one is to construct a tool independently by the researcher and the second one is to select a standardized tool that is already available in the field of study.

The tool used in the present study is Indian Adaptation of Bell's Adjustment Inventory, constructed and standardized by Lalita Sharma.

The tool was administered on a small sample of teacher educators and found that this tool is useful to the present study as per the norms and values of the tool.

ADMINISTRATION OF THE TOOL

The tool was administered personally by the researcher on the teacher educators and the sample was asked to respond to the statements. Before giving the tool to the participants, the researcher explained the purpose of the present investigation. Directions given on the cover sheet were read out to the participants and scientific instructions were given. The teacher educators attended to the scale very well.

4

Analysis of Data

"The analysis and interpretation of data, involve the objective material in the possession of the research and his subjective reaction and desires to drive from the data the inherent meanings in their relation to the problem."

—Francis Rummel

Analysis of data is the most skilled task of all stages of research. It depends on the judgement and skill of the researcher. Analysis of data means studying the tabulated material in order to determine inherent facts or meanings. It involves breaking down complex factors into simple ones and putting the parts in new arrangements for the purpose of interpretation.

The first step in the analysis of data is critical examination of the assembled data. This includes the researcher to think and analyze the data in the next method of analysis, i.e., coding. Coding means assigning of symbols to each response, the purpose of which is to translate raw data into symbols. This depends on the proper coding of responses. Coding can be done by the respondent or observer or the interviewer. There may be difficulties in coding due to inadequacy of data, inefficiency of the coder and lack of editing or scrutinizing the available data. Editing can be helpful for coding and for improving the quality of data collection.

Tabulation is means recording classification in a compact form in such a way so as to facilitate comparisons. Data are arranged in rows and columns to facilitate mathematical and statistical operations. It is of great help in the analysis and interpretation of data. While tabulating the data, the purpose of the study has to be kept in mind.

The method of analysis chosen for a particular study depends upon the nature of objectives, hypotheses to be tested, the purpose and use of the study statistical methods are the mathematical techniques used to facilitate the interpretation of numerical data secured from groups of individuals or group of observations or a single individual. A basic knowledge about statistics becomes inevitable for research workers for systematic analysis and accurate and precise interpretation of data.

For the present study titled "Adjustment and Teacher Educators", several statistical techniques were used to perform the analysis. After collecting the data from teacher educators through a standardized tool, the analysis was performed keeping in view the objectives framed, hypotheses formulated, type of tool used, etc. For this purpose Mean, SD, Critical Ratio, etc., were employed. The highest or the lowest adjustment score one can get is 42 or 0 respectively. The higher the value of the sampling unit the lesser the adjustment and the lower the value of the sampling unit the higher the adjustment, as per the inventory.

Adjustment of Teacher Educators

Hypothesis 1: Teacher educators are not having high adjustment

To test the validity of the hypothesis 1, the mean of adjustment scores was calculated (Table 4.1).

Table 4.1

Adjustment of Teacher Educators

Sample	Sample Size	Mean	Standard Deviation
Whole	130	20.15	5.23

From the mean value of Table 4.1, it is evident that there was high level of adjustment in teacher educators.

The hypothesis that "teacher educators not having high adjustment" can be rejected as the teacher educators are possessing a high level of adjustment.

Adjustment and Gender

Hypothesis 2: There is no significant difference between the adjustment of men and women teacher educators.

To test the validity of the hypothesis 2, the following calculations were carried out (Table 4.2).

Table 4.2

Comparison of Adjustment among Men and Women Teacher Educators

Variable	Sample	Mean Size	S.D	Mean	df Difference	Critical Ratio
Men	70	20.53	4.87	0.8	0.92	0.86 ×
Women	60	19.73	5.51			

Critical Value at 0.05 level = 1.96.

× *Not Significant at 0.05 level.*

From the value of Table 4.2, it is evident that both men and women teacher educators were with a high level of adjustment without any significant difference between them.

The hypothesis that "there is no significant difference between the adjustment of men and women teacher educators" can be accepted as there is no significant difference in the level of adjustment of men and women teacher educators.

Adjustment and Locality

Hypothesis 3: There is no significant difference between the adjustment of rural and urban teacher educators.

To test the validity of the hypothesis 3, the following calculations were carried out (Table 4.3).

Table 4.3

Comparison of Adjustment among Rural and Urban Teacher Educators

Variable	*Sample*	*Mean Size*	*S.D.*	*Mean*	*df Difference*	*Critical Ratio*
Rural	64	22.28	5.38			
				4.21	0.84	5.01*
Urban	66	18.07	4.14			

Critical Value at 0.05 level = 1.96.

* *Significant at 0.05 level.*

From the values of Table 4.3, it is evident that both rural and urban teacher educators were with a high level of adjustment with a significant difference between them. The urban teacher educators were more adjusted than the rural teacher educators.

The hypothesis that "there is no significant difference between the adjustment of rural and urban teacher educators" can be rejected

Adjustment and Management

Hypothesis 4: There is no significant difference between the adjustment of aided and unaided teacher educators.

To test the validity of the hypothesis 4, the following calculations were made (Table 4.4).

Table 4.4

Comparison of Adjustment among Aided and Unaided Teacher Educators

Variable	Sample	Mean Size	S.D.	Mean	df Difference	Critical Ratio
Aided	12	17.17	4.12	3.28	1.33	2.47*
Unaided	118	20.45	5.20			

Critical Value at 0.05 level = 1.96.

* *Significant at 0.05 level.*

From the value of Table 4.4, it is evident that both aided and unaided teacher educators were with a high level of adjustment with significant difference between them. Aided college teacher educators were having more adjustment level than their counterparts.

The hypothesis that "there is no significant difference between the adjustment of aided and unaided teacher educators" can be rejected as there is significant difference in the level of adjustment of aided and unaided teacher educators.

Adjustment and ExperienceHypothesis 5: Adjustment and Experience

Hypothesis 5: There is no significant difference between the adjustment of teacher educators of experience below 15 years and above 15 years.

To test the validity of the hypothesis 5, the following calculations were made (Table 4.5).

From the values of Table 4.5, it is evident that both high and less experience teacher educators were with a high level of adjustment with significant difference between them. The highly experienced teacher educators were with more adjustment than the less experienced teacher educators.

Table 4.5

Comparison of Adjustment among High (Above 15 Years) Experience and Less (Below 15 Years) Experience Teacher Educators

Variable	*Sample*	*Mean Size*	*S.D.*	*Mean*	*df Difference*	*Critical Ratio*
High Experience	29	17.10	4.20	3.91	0.94	4.15*
Less Experience	101	21.01	5.13			

Critical Value at 0.05 level = 1.96.

* *Significant at 0.05 level.*

The hypothesis that "there is no significant difference between the adjustment of teacher educators of experience below 15 years and above 15 years" can be rejected as there is a significant difference in the level of adjustment of high and less experienced teacher educators.

Adjustment and Age

Hypothesis 6: There is no significant difference between the adjustment of teacher educators of age below 45 years and above 45 years.

To test the validity of the hypothesis 6, the following calculations were made (Table 4.6).

Table 4.6

Comparison of Adjustment among Teacher Educators of Age Above 45 Years and Below 45 Years

Variable	*Sample*	*Mean Size*	*S.D.*	*Mean Difference*	*df*	*Critical Ratio*
Above 45 Yrs.	25	17.64	4.16	3.1	0.87	3.56*
Below 45 Yrs.	105	20.74	5.25			

Critical Value at 0.05 level = 1.96.

* *Significant at 0.05 level.*

From the values of Table 4.6, it is evident that both the teacher educators of age above 45 years, below 45 years with a high level of adjustment with a significant difference between them. The aged ones were with a higher level of adjustment than their counterparts.

The hypothesis that "there is no significant difference between the adjustment of teacher educators of age below 45 years and above 45 years" can be rejected as there is significant difference in the level of adjustment of teacher educators of aged above 45 years and below 45 years.

5

Summary, Conclusions and Discussion

"Research is perhaps the only assurance we have that a discipline or a procession will not decay into meaningless scraps of dogmatic utterance".

—Bruce W. Fuckcman

SUMMARY

The concept of adjustment is as old as human race on earth. The systematic emergence of this concept starts from Darwin's (1859) *Theory of Evolution*. During early days, the concept was purely biological and Darwin used the term as adaptation. Most of the biologists use the term adaptation strictly for physical demands of the environment, but the psychologists use the term adjustment for varying conditions of social or interpersonal relations in the society.

Thus the concept of adjustment is not a new one. It is one of those terms in Psychology that has been a source of great confusion as the word has many meanings packed into it.

We see that adjustment means reactions to the demands and pressures of social environment imposed upon the individual. The demands may be external (e.g. environment) or internal (e.g. hunger, water, air, sleep etc.) to which the individual has to react. These two types of demands sometimes clash with each other and consequently make the adjustment a complicated process for the individual.

Psychologists have interpreted adjustment from two important point of view: one adjustment as an achievement and another, adjustment as a process. The first point of view emphasizes the quality or efficiency of an individual where he can perform his duties in different circumstances and the second lays emphasis on the process by which an individual adjusts in his external environment. The term adjustment refers to a harmonious relationship between the individual and the environment. Piaget (1952) used the terms accommodation and assimilation to represent the alternations of oneself or environment as a means of adjustment. "Adjustment would be a harmonious relationship of an individual to his environment which affords him comfortable life devoid of strain, stress, conflict and frustration". (Rao, 1990)

A satisfactory relationship may mean adaptation to the demands of reality. A biological view of adjustment would emphasize adoption for survival, while a narrower view of it would be adoption for need reduction. The efforts of the individual to adapt himself to the environment, to over come frustration in achieving the gratification of his needs, may be called the adjustment process. The situation that offers few frustrating barriers to the individual would be favourable and aids adjustment. The adjustment process is affected and modified by the individual's experiences and thus learning plays a significant part in aiding adjustment.

Adjustment involves effective adaptation. It consists in the reduction of inner needs, stresses and strains, in this sense, adjustment could be a unique pattern depending upon the personality and the needs of the individual. As each individual differs, so his needs differ and consequently his adjustment differs. Adjustment is actually a condition or a state of mind and behaviour in which one feels that one's needs have been, or will be, gratified. The satisfaction of these needs, however, must lie within the framework and requirements of one's culture and society. As long as this happens, the individual remains adjusted; failing this he may drift towards maladjustment and mental illness.

The present study is intended to find out the level of adjustment of teacher educators. The sample was drawn from the teacher educators working in Colleges of Education situated in Krishna, Guntur and Srikakulam districts. The sample size chosen for the present study was 130 teacher educators.

The objectives of the study were to find out the adjustment of teacher educators, to compare the adjustment of male and female teacher educators, to compare the adjustment of rural and urban teacher educators, to compare the adjustment of aided and unaided Teacher educators, to compare the adjustment of teacher educators of aged below 45 years and above 45 years, and to compare the adjustment of teacher educators of having experience below 15 years and above 15 years.

The normative survey method was used for this study. This method investigates into the conditions and relationships that exist at present in the context of adjustment.

For the present study, the following variables were chosen

Gender (men and women teacher educators), Locality (rural and urban teacher educators), Management of the college (aided and unaided), Experience (experience below 15 years and above 15 years), and Age (age below 45 years and above 45 years).

Hypotheses formulated for the present study were teacher educators not having high adjustment, there is no significant difference between the adjustment of men and women teacher educators, there is no significant difference between the adjustment of rural and urban teacher educators, there is no significant difference between the adjustment of aided and unaided teacher educators, there is no significant difference between the adjustment of teacher educators with experience below 15 years and above 15 years, and there is no significant difference between the adjustment of teacher educators of aged below 45 years and above 45 years.

A sample is a small group which represents all the traits and characteristics of the population. The teacher educators working in Colleges of Education of Krishna, Guntur and Srikakulam districts were selected as population. The stratified random sampling technique was used in selecting the sample. The size of the sample was 130 teacher educators.

A research tool is a tool used for the purpose of data collection. The tool used in the present study was Indian Adaptation of Bell's Adjustment Inventory, constructed and standardized by Dr. Sharma.

For the analysis of data, suitable statistical techniques like mean, S.D. and critical ratio were used.

CONCLUSIONS AND DISCUSSION

From the analysis of the data, the following conclusions are drawn and these are followed by necessary discussion

1. **The Teacher educators were holding a high level of adjustment.**

The above result was not supported by Goyal, J.C. (1980).

The present status of adjustment may be due to the environment or atmosphere of the colleges where the teacher educators work. This may be due to the healthy conditions surrounded by them. Teacher educators may develop further the adjustment by participating in social activities, by participating in yoga and meditation by developing sympathy and empathy, and by trying to understand others.

2. The men and women teacher educators had a high level of adjustment without any significant difference between them.

The above result was supported by the studies of Nomani (1965), Baral (1969), Mankad (1982), Chadda (1985), Gaur (1985), Shahpur (2004), Vamadevappa (2005), Sabu and Jangaiah (2005) and contradicted by Prasad (1985), Shirotriya (1988, Subrahmanian (1989) and Rather (1990).

Because of the same mental maturity, personality, surrounding environment, aspirations and attitudes, etc., might have played their legitimate role in having no significant difference in the level of adjustment by men and women teacher educators.

Both men and women teacher educators should identify their position in teaching arena in order to improve further their adjustment, and develop life skills, coping strategies and accepting the conditions in realistic view for better adjustment.

3. The rural and urban teacher educators hold a high level of adjustment with a significant difference between them. The urban teacher educators were more adjusted than rural ones.

The above results was supported by Sharma (1979), Pandey (1979), Saun (1980), Kumar, Sushma (1990), Gupta, Sharma (1990) and contradicted by Nomani (1965), Chadda (1985) and Kumari (1988).

As the teacher educators of rural and urban localities strive equally for better adjustment, hey should enhance the level of adjustment by following adjustment mechanisms in every talk of life.

4. The aided and unaided teacher educators possessed a high level of adjustment with a significant difference between them. The aided staff were with more adjustment level than their counterparts.

The above result was supported by Gaur, Ashwani Kumar (1985), Gupta (1990) and Surekha (2008).

As there was mush difference in the facilities provided by both aided and unaided colleges of Education. The teacher educators of aided colleges feel secure than the teacher educators of unaided colleges. Due to this cause only there is a significant difference in the level of adjustment. But overall the adjustment of teacher educators of aided and unaided colleges is very unsatisfactory.

5. **High and low experienced teacher educators possessed a high level of adjustment with a significant difference between them. The highly experienced teacher educators were with higher level of adjustment than the less experienced teacher educators.**

The above result was supported by Sabu and Jangaiah (2005) and contradicted by Donga (1987).

As there was much difference in the theoretical and practical experience of life, the experienced teacher educators with their exposure to various phenomena in life and classrooms, they have higher level of adjustment than their counterparts. Both of them should further enhance their adjustment levels and support their prospective teachers in developing proper adjustment.

6. **Teacher educators aged above 45 years and below 45 years had a high level of adjustment with a significant difference between them. The aged were with better adjustment than others.**

The above result was supported by Jamuna (1985), Subrahmanian (1989) and contradicted by Donga (1987), Goyal and Chopra (1989), Sabu and jangaiah (2005).

The young teacher educators possess intensions, anxieties, emotions and aspirations at a very high level. At this time if they face any situation against to their will, they are not able to set or receive the condition positively. This may arise adjustment problems. But these intensions, anxieties, emotions and aspirations are slow down with age, and they can receive them in a healthy way and they either accept or try to accept the conditions positively. So, there is a significant difference in the level of adjustment. But the level of adjustment of junior and senior teacher educators should be similar so that they can mould the student teachers as well adjusted individuals.

7. **The teacher educator working in Colleges of Education are with high level of adjustment. Except gender, the locality, the management of the college, the experience and the age of the teacher educators did show their influence on the level of adjustment of teacher educators.**

The teacher educators should identify the reasons for better adjustment and should attend to those by which they can enhance or at least maintain the same level of adjustment. Better skills, good relations with colleagues will help the teacher educators in improving the adjustment. Relaxation techniques, yoga and meditation, better study habits, good life skills, appropriate aspirations, etc., may also help in improving the adjustment level of teacher educators.

SUGGESTIONS FOR FURTHER RESEARCH

The present study, A study of Adjustment of Teacher Educators, brings to light a good number of new areas to be studied by future researchers. The areas and variables that are not covered by this study may be put to test to enlighten the other associated factors. So, the researchers may think of the following areas of study in detail.

1. This study can be extended to students of Intermediate, Graduation and Post-graduation at district and State levels.

2. This study can also be extended to the secondary school teachers, junior college lecturers, degree college lecturers and university teachers at university, district and State levels.

3. Research can be taken up to know the effect of factors like marital status, social and economic conditions, frustration and other personality factors on adjustment.

4. Studies can be considered to know the impact of emotional stability, drives, aggressiveness, stress, etc., on the adjustment.
5. Studies can be taken up to know the influence of adjustment on creativity, academic achievement, scholastic performance, attitudes, etc.
6. Studies may be taken up in different areas of adjustment separately (personal adjustment, home adjustment, social adjustment, emotional adjustment).
7. Studies may be taken up to identify the relationship between various psychological factors and adjustment.

Bibliography

Aggarwal, J.C. (1996). *Essentials of Educational Psychology*. New Delhi: Vikas Publishing House Private Limited.

Aggrwal, J.C. (2004). *Essentials of Educational Psychology*. New Delhi: Vikas Publishing House Private Limited.

Best, John W. and James V. Khan (2005). *Research in Education*, 9th edition. New Delhi: Prentice-Hall of India Private Limited.

Bhatia, K.K. and P. Yakaiah (2003). *Introduction to Educational Psychology*. New Delhi: Kalyani Publishers.

Buch, M.B., Editor. *Third Survey of Research in Education (1978-1983)*. Baroda: CASE, M.S. University of Baroda.

Buch, M.B., (Editor). *Fourth Survey of Research in Education (1983-1988)*. New Delhi: NCERT.

Buch, M.B., (Editor). *Fifth Survey of Research in Education (1988-1992)*. New Delhi: NCERT.

Chaube, S.P. (2002). *Educational Psychology and Educational Statistics*. Agra: Educational Publishers.

Chuhan, S.S. (1983). *Psychology of Adolescence.* New Delhi: Allied Publishers Private Limited.

Crow and Crow (1979). *Educational Psychology.* New Delhi: Eurasia Publishing House Private Limited.

Dandapani, S. (2001). *Advanced Educational Psychology.* New Delhi: Anmol Publications Private Limited.

Dash, M., and Neena Dash (2006). *Fundamentals of Educational Psychology*. New Delhi: Atlantic Publishers.

Dosajh, N.L. (1982). *Advanced Educational Psychology.* New Delhi: Allied Publishers Private Limited.

Elizabeth B. Hurlock (1983). *Developmental Psychology*. New Delhi: Tata McGraw-Hill Publishing Company Limited.

Govind, Tiwari (1984). *Abnormal Psychology.* Agra: Vinod Pustak Mandir.

Jayaswal, S.R. (1964). *Foundations of Educational Psychology.* Lucknow: Prakashan Kendra.

Kakkar, S.B. (1989). *Educational Psychology and Guidance.* Ambala Cantt: The Indian Publications.

Kaur, Gurvinder (September 2007), "Marital Adjustment Problems Faced by Non-working Women and Working Women Teachers". *Edutracks,* Vol.7, No.1, pp. 26-27.

Kundu, C.L., and D.N. Tutoo (1985). *Educational Psychology.* New Delhi: Sterling Publishers Private Limited.

Mangal, S.K. (1984). *Abnormal Psychology.* New Delhi: Sterling Publishers Private Limited.

Mangal, S.K. (1999). *Advanced Educational Psychology.* New Delhi: Prentice-Hall of India Private Limited.

Parameswaran, E.G. and C. Beena (1988). *Invitation to Psychology*. New Delhi: Tata McGraw Hill Publishing Company Limited.

Prasadh, R. Siva (Jan-March, 2005), "Adjustment and Achievement of Residential School Students". *New Frontiers in Education,* Vol. XXXV, No. 1, pp. 55-58.

Rachana, Sharma (2004). *Abnormal Psychology.* New Delhi: Atlantic Publishers and Distributors.

Rai, B.C. (1983). *Educational Psychology.* Lucknow: Prakashan Kendra.

Rao, S. Narayana (1990). *Educational Psychology.* New Delhi: Wiley Eastern Limited.

Reddy, I.V. Ramana (1983). *Psychological Foundations of Education.* Tirupathi: Veni Publishers.

Sharma, Ram Nath and R.K. Sharma (2006). *Advanced Educational Psychology.* New Delhi: Atlantic Publishers.

Srivastava, D.N. (1985). *General Psychology.* Agra: Vinod Pustak Mandir.

Subbu. S. and C. Jangaiah (September 2005), "Adjustment and Teachers' Stress". *Edutracks,* Vol. 5, No. 1, pp. 32-35.

Surekha (March 2008), "Relationship between Students Adjustment and Academic Achievement", *Edutracks,* Vol. 7, No. 7, pp. 26-31.

Vamadevappa, H.V. (Jan-March, 2005). "Adjustment of Over Achievers and Under Achievers in Biology". New Frontiers in Education, Vol. XXXV, No. 1, pp. 46-49.

Virginia Nichols and Quinn (1985). *Applying Psychology.* Singapore: Library of Congress Cataloging in Publications.

Additional Reading

Bhaskara Rao, Digumarti (1994). *Scientific Aptitude.* New Delhi: Ashish Publishing House.

Bhaskara Rao, Digumarti (1995). *Animal Kingdom.* New Delhi: Discovery Publishing House. ISBN 81-7141-274-2.

Bhaskara Rao, Digumarti (1995). *Batracology.* New Delhi: Discovery Publishing House. ISBN 81-7141-279-3.

Bhaskara Rao, Digumarti (1997). *Scientific Attitude.* New Delhi: Discovery Publishing House. ISBN 81-7141-381-1.

Bhaskara Rao, Digumarti (1996). *Scientific Attitude vis-à-vis Scientific Aptitude.* New Delhi: Discovery Publishing House. ISBN 81-7141-308-0.

Bhaskara Rao, Digumarti (2004). *Scientific Attitude, Scientific Aptitude and Achievement.* New Delhi: Discovery Publishing House. ISBN 81-7141-781-7.

Bhaskara Rao, Digumarti (2004). *Educational Administration.* New Delhi: Discovery Publishing House. ISBN 81-7141-842-2.

Bhaskara Rao, Digumarti (2004). *Issues in School Education.* New Delhi: Discovery Publishing House. ISBN 81-8356-025-3.

Bhaskara Rao, Digumarti, editor (1996). *Encyclopaedia of Education For All*, 5 volumes. New Delhi: APH Publishing Corporation. ISBN 81-7024-759-4 (set).

Vol. I *Education For All: The World Conference.* ISBN 81-7024-760-8

Vol. II *Education For All: The EPA-9 Summit.* ISBN 81-7024-761-6

Vol. III *Education For All: Quality Education For All.* ISBN 81-7024-762-6.

Vol. IV *Education For All: Planning and Monitoring.* ISBN 81-7024-763-4.

Vol. V *Education For All: The Indian Scenario.* ISBN 81-7024-764-0.

Bhaskara Rao, Digumarti, editor (1996). *National Policy on Education,* 2 volumes. New Delhi: Anmol Publications Pvt. Ltd. ISBN 81-7488-323-1.

Bhaskara Rao, Digumarti, editor (1996). *Global Perceptions on Peace Education,* 3 volumes. New Delhi: Discovery Publishing House. ISBN 81-7141-319-6.

Bhaskara Rao, Digumarti, editor (1997). *Education for the 21st Century.* New Delhi: Discovery Publishing House. ISBN 81-7141-389-7.

Bhaskara Rao, Digumarti, editor (1997). *Reflections on Scientific Attitude.* New Delhi: Discovery Publishing House. ISBN 81-7141-319-6.

Bhaskara Rao, Digumarti, editor (1997). *Success Story of a Primary Education Project.* New Delhi: APH Publishing Corporation. ISBN 81-7024-850-7.

Bhaskara Rao, Digumarti, editor (1997). *World Food Summit.* New Delhi: Discovery Publishing House. ISBN 81-7141-386-2.

Bhaskara Rao, Digumarti, editor (1997). *Care the Child,* 2 Volumes. New Delhi: Discovery Publishing House. ISBN 81-7141-394-3.

Bhaskara Rao, Digumarti, editor (1998). *Earth Summit,* 2 Volumes. New Delhi: Discovery Publishing House. ISBN 81-7141-435-4.

Bhaskara Rao, Digumarti, editor (1998). *Adolescence Education.* New Delhi: Discovery Publishing House. ISBN 81-7141-432-X.

Bhaskara Rao, Digumarti, editor (1998). *Community and School Nutrition Education.* New Delhi: Discovery Publishing House. ISBN 81-7141-435-4.

Bhaskara Rao, Digumarti, editor (1998). *District Primary Education Programme.* New Delhi: Discovery Publishing House. ISBN 81-7141-396-X.

Bhaskara Rao, Digumarti, editor (1998). *National Policy on Education: Towards an Enlightened and Humane Society.* New Delhi: Discovery Publishing House. ISBN 81-7141-426-5.

Bhaskara Rao, Digumarti, editor (1998). *Reforming School Education.* New Delhi: Discovery Publishing House. ISBN 81-7141-403-6.

Bhaskara Rao, Digumarti, editor (1998). *Teacher Education in India.* New Delhi: Discovery Publishing House. ISBN 81-7141-406-0.

Bhaskara Rao, Digumarti, editor (1998). *World Summit for Social Development.* New Delhi: Discovery Publishing House. ISBN 81-7141-420-6.

Bhaskara Rao, Digumarti, editor (1999). *International Encyclopaedia of AIDS*, 11 Volumes. New Delhi: Discovery Publishing House. ISBN 81-7141-522-6 (set).

Vol. 1 *Introduction to HIV/AIDS*. ISBN 81-7141-523-7.

Vol. 2 *HIV/AIDS – Issues and Challenges*, 2 parts. ISBN 81-7141-524-5.

Vol. 3 *HIV/AIDS – Socio Economic Realities*. ISBN 81-7141-524-3.

Vol. 4 *HIV/AIDS – Law Ethics and Human Rights*, 2 parts. ISBN 81-7141-526-1.

Vol. 5 *AIDS and NGOs*. ISBN 81-7141-527-X.

Vol. 6 *AIDS and Home Care*. ISBN 81-7141-528-8.

Vol. 7 *STD Case Management*. ISBN 81-7141-529-6.

Vol. 8 *HIV/AIDS Prevention and Care – Teaching Modules for Nurses and Midwives*. ISBN 81-7141-530-X.

Vol. 9 *HIV Prevention Education for Educational Institutions*. ISBN 81-7141-531-8.

Vol.10 *Instructional Modules for AIDS Education*. ISBN 81-7141-532-6.

Vol.11 *School Health Education to prevent AIDS and STD – A Package for Curriculum Planners*. ISBN 81-7141-533-4.

Bhaskara Rao, Digumarti, editor (2000). *International Encyclopaedia of Human Rights*, 7 volumes in 13 parts. New Delhi: Discovery Publishing House. ISBN 81-7141-567-9 (set).

Vol. 1 *International Instruments of Human Rights*, 2 parts. ISBN 81-7141-569-4.

Vol. 2 *Regional Instruments of Human Rights*. ISBN 81-7141-604-7.

Vol. 3 *Human Rights and the United Nations*, 2 parts. ISBN 81-7141-605-5.

Vol. 4 *Fact Files of Human Rights*, 3 parts. ISBN 81-7141-606-3.

Vol. 5 *Study Stories of Human Rights,* 3 parts. ISBN 81-7141-607-3.

Vol. 6 *International Meetings on Human Rights*, 2 parts. ISBN 81-714-608-X.

Vol. 7 *Professional Training in Human Rights*. ISBN 81-7141-609-8.

Bhaskara Rao, Digumarti, editor (2000). *International Encyclopaedia of Science and Technology Education*, 11 volumes. New Delhi: Discovery Publishing House. ISBN 81-7141-548-2 (set).

Vol. 1 *Science and Technology Education.* ISBN 81-7141-568-7.

Vol. 2 *Science Education in Developing Countries.* ISBN 81-7141-569-9.

Vol. 3 *Organizational Structure of Science.* ISBN 81-7141-570-9.

Vol. 4 *Science Education in Asia and the Pacific.* ISBN 81-7141-571-7

Vol. 5 *Science and Technology Education For All.* ISBN 81-7141-572-5.

Vol. 6 *Values, Ethics, Talent and Girls in Science and Technology Education.* ISBN 81-7141-573-3.

Vol. 7 *Popularization of Science and Technology Education.* ISBN 81-7141-574-1.

Vol. 8 *Science, Power and Society.* ISBN 81-7141-575-X.

Vol. 9 *Information Technology.* ISBN 81-7141-576-8.

Vol.10 *Teacher Training in Science and Technology Education.* ISBN 81-7142-577-6.

Vol.11 *Teacher Training in Science and Technology: A Curriculum Framework.* ISBN 81-7141-578-4.

Bhaskara Rao, Digumarti, editor (2000). *Education For All: Achieving the Goal*, 3 volumes. New Delhi: APH Publishing Corporation. ISBN 81-7648-152-1 (set).

Vol. I *The Global Consensus.* ISBN 81-7648-155-6.

Vol. II *Mid-Decade Review Reports of Regional Seminars.* ISBN 81-7648- 154-8.

Vol. III *Issues and Trends.* ISBN 81-7648-155-6.

Bhaskara Rao, Digumarti, editor (2001). *Nuclear Materials: Issues and Concerns*, 2 volumes. New Delhi: Discovery Publishing House. ISBN 81-7141-611-X.

Bhaskara Rao, Digumarti, editor (2001). *Distance Education in Different Countries.* New Delhi: APH Publishing Corporation. ISBN 81-7648-229-3.

Bhaskara Rao, Digumarti, editor (2001). *Decentralised Management of Education: Management of Education in Panchayati Raj and Municipal Bodies.* New Delhi: Discovery Publishing House. ISBN 81-7141-617-9.

Bhaskara Rao, Digumarti, editor (2001). *Electrochemistry for Environmental Protection.* New Delhi: Discovery Publishing House. ISBN 81-7141-619-5.

Bhaskara Rao, Digumarti, editor (2001). *Global Educational Studies.* New Delhi: Discovery Publishing House. ISBN 81-7141-616-0.

Bhaskara Rao, Digumarti, editor (2001). *Global Synthesis of Educational Assessment.* New Delhi: Discovery Publishing House. ISBN 81-7141-613-6.

Bhaskara Rao, Digumarti, editor (2001). *Jomtein Decade of Education.* New Delhi: Discovery Publishing House. ISBN 81-7141-618-7.

Bhaskara Rao, Digumarti, editor (2001). *World Conference on Education for All.* New Delhi: APH Publishing Corporation. ISBN 81-7141-274-9.

Bhaskara Rao, Digumarti, editor (2001). *World Conference on Higher Education.* New Delhi: Discovery Publishing House. ISBN 81-7141-610-1.

Bhaskara Rao, Digumarti, editor (2001). *World Conference on Science.* New Delhi: Discovery Publishing House. ISBN 81-7141-612-8.

Bhaskara Rao, Digumarti, editor (2003). *Inspiring Experiences in Teacher Education*. New Delhi: Discovery Publishing House. ISBN 81-7141-656-X.

Bhaskara Rao, Digumarti, editor (2003). *International Studies in Education*, 3 volumes. New Delhi: Discovery Publishing House. ISBN 81-7141-647-0.

Bhaskara Rao, Digumarti, editor (2003). *Military Conversion: Impact on Science and Technology*. New Delhi: Discovery Publishing House. ISBN 81-7141-578-4.

Bhaskara Rao, Digumarti, editor (2003). *United Nations Millennium Summit*. New Delhi: Discovery Publishing House. ISBN 81-7141-632-2.

Bhaskara Rao, Digumarti, editor (2003). *World Assembly on Aging*. New Delhi: Discovery Publishing House. ISBN 81-7141-637-3.

Bhaskara Rao, Digumarti, editor (2003). *World Conference on Human Rights*. New Delhi: Discovery Publishing House. ISBN 81-7141-661-6.

Bhaskara Rao, Digumarti, editor (2003). *World Education Forum*. New Delhi: Discovery Publishing House. ISBN 81-7141-639-X.

Bhaskara Rao, Digumarti, editor (2003). *Education, Employment and Human Resource Development*. New Delhi: Discovery Publishing House. ISBN 81-7141- 681-0.

Bhaskara Rao, Digumarti, editor (2003). *Successful Schooling*. New Delhi: Discovery Publishing House. ISBN 81-7141-677-2.

Bhaskara Rao, Digumarti, editor (2003). *European Education and Teachers*. New Delhi: Discovery Publishing House. ISBN 81-7141-702-7.

Bhaskara Rao, Digumarti, editor (2003). *Teachers in a Changing World*. New Delhi: Discovery Publishing House. ISBN 81-7141-694-2.

Bhaskara Rao, Digumarti, editor (2004). *International Guidelines on Open and Distance Teacher Education*. New Delhi: Discovery Publishing House. ISBN 81-7141-777-9.

Bhaskara Rao, Digumarti, editor (2004). *Adult Learning in the 21st Century*. New Delhi: Discovery Publishing House. ISBN 81-7141-797-3.

Bhaskara Rao, Digumarti, editor (2004). *Educational Practices: Research and Recommendations*. New Delhi: Discovery Publishing House. ISBN 81-7141-835-X.

Bhaskara Rao, Digumarti, editor (2004). *General Secondary Education In the 21st Century*. New Delhi: Discovery Publishing House.

Bhaskara Rao, Digumarti, editor (2004). *International Encyclopaedia of Learning to Live Together*, 4 volumes. New Delhi: Discovery Publishing House. ISBN 81-7141-848-1.

Vol. 1 *International Conference on Learning to Live Together.*

Vol. 2 *Globalization and Living Together.*

Vol. 3 *Curriculum for Learning to Live Together.*

Vol. 4 *Science Education for the Contemporary Society.*

Bhaskara Rao, Digumarti, editor (2004). *Reforming Secondary Education*. New Delhi: Discovery Publishing House. ISBN 81-7141-843-0.

Bhaskara Rao, Digumarti, editor (2004). *Human Rights Education*. New Delhi: Discovery Publishing House. ISBN 81-7141-882-1.

Bhaskara Rao, Digumarti, editor (2004). *United Nations Decade for Human Rights Education*. New Delhi: Discovery Publishing House. ISBN 81-7141- 887-2.

Bhaskara Rao, Digumarti, editor (2004). *Technical and Vocational Education and Training in the 21st Century*. New Delhi: Discovery Publishing House. ISBN 81-7141-984-4.

Bhaskara Rao, Digumarti, editor (2005). *Encyclopaedia of Education For All*, 5 volumes. New Delhi: Discovery Publishing House.

Bhaskara Rao, Digumarti and B.S.V. Dutt, editors (2003). *Education: Programmes and Policies*. New Delhi: APH Publishing Corporation. ISBN 81-7648-470-9.

Bhaskara Rao, Digumarti, C.A.P. Swamy and B.S.V. Dutt (1997). *Self-Evaluation in Student Teaching*. New Delhi: Discovery Publishing House. ISBN 81-7141-374-9.

Bhaskara Rao, Digumarti and D. Naresh Kumar (2004). *School Teacher Effectiveness*. New Delhi: Discovery Publishing House. ISBN 81-7141-782-5.

Bhaskara Rao, Digumarti and D. Sridhar (2002). *Job Satisfaction of School Teachers*. New Delhi: Discovery Publishing House. ISBN 81-7141-652-7.

Bhaskara Rao, Digumarti, C. Sridevi and K. Vijaya (1995). *Achievement in Social Studies*. New Delhi: Discovery Publishing House. ISBN 81-7141-281-5.

Bhaskara Rao, Digumarti and Digumarti Pushpa Latha (1994). *Achievement in Biology*. New Delhi: Discovery Publishing House. ISBN 81-7141-264-5.

Bhaskara Rao, Digumarti and Digumarti Pushpa Latha (1995). *Achievement in English*. New Delhi: Discovery Publishing House. ISBN 81-7141-283-1.

Bhaskara Rao, Digumarti and Digumarti Pushpa Latha (1994). *Achievement in Science*. New Delhi: Discovery Publishing House. ISBN 81-7141-280-70.

Bhaskara Rao, Digumarti and Digumarti Pushpa Latha (1995). *Achievement in Mathematics*. New Delhi: Discovery Publishing House. ISBN 81-7141-278-5.

Bhaskara Rao, Digumarti and Digumarti Pushpa Latha (2004). *Education for Women*. New Delhi: Discovery Publishing House. ISBN 81-7141-873-2.

Bhaskara Rao, Digumarti, Digumarti Pushpa Latha and Digumarthi Harshitha, editors (2001). *Biological Warfare*. New Delhi: Discovery Publishing House. ISBN 81-7141-597-0.

Bhaskara Rao, Digumarti, Digumarti Pushpa Latha and Digumarthi Harshitha, editors (2001). *Women as Educators*. New Delhi: Discovery Publishing House. ISBN 81-7141-602-0.

Bhaskara Rao, Digumarti and Digumarthi Harshitha (2004). *Adjustment of Adolescents*. New Delhi: APH Publishing House. ISBN 81-7648-836-8.

Bhaskara Rao, Digumarti and Digumarthi Harshitha, editors (2001). *Education in India*. New Delhi: APH Publishing House. ISBN 81-7648-207-2.

Bhaskara Rao, Digumarti and Digumarti Pushpa Latha, editors (1998). *International Encyclopaedia of Women,* 5 volumes. New Delhi: Discovery Publishing House. ISBN 81-7141-410-9 (set).

Vol. 1 *Status of World's Women*. ISBN 81-7141-494-X.

Vol. 2 *Women, Education and Empowerment*. ISBN 81-7141-498-1.

Vol. 3 *Women Challenges and Advancement*. ISBN 81-7141-497-4.

Vol. 4 *Women and Family Health*. ISBN 81-7141-497-4.

Vol. 5 *Women and International Action*. ISBN 81-7141-498-2.

Bhaskara Rao, Digumarti, Digumarti Pushpa Latha and Digumarthi Harshitha, editors (2001). *Assessing Learning Achievement*. New Delhi: Discovery Publishing House. ISBN 81-7141-601-2.

Bhaskara Rao, Digumarti, Digumarti Pushpa Latha and Digumarthi Harshitha, editors (2001). *Energy Security*. New Delhi: Discovery Publishing House. ISBN 81-7141-598-9.

Bhaskara Rao, Digumarti, Digumarthi Harshitha and K.R.S. Sambasiva Rao, editors (1999). *Advanced Biotechnology.* New Delhi: Discovery Publishing House. ISBN 81-7141-516-4.

Bhaskara Rao, Digumarti and K.R.S. Sambasiva Rao, editors (1996). *Current Trends in Indian Education.* New Delhi: Discovery Publishing House. ISBN 81-7141-311-0.

Bhaskara Rao, Digumarti and E. Sreekanth Babu (2004). *Educational Interests of School Students.* New Delhi: Discovery Publishing House. ISBN 81-7141-837-6.

Bhaskara Rao, Digumarti and K. Vijaya (1995). *A Text Book Evaluation.* Ambala Cantt: The Associated Publishers.

Bhaskara Rao, Digumarti and M.A. Fayaz (2004). *Problems of Primary School Drop-outs.* New Delhi: Discovery Publishing House. ISBN 81-7141- 834-1.

Bhaskara Rao, Digumarti and N.V.M. Mohana Rao (2002). *Problems of Mentally Handicapped Children.* New Delhi: Discovery Publishing House. ISBN 81-7141- 645-4.

Bhaskara Rao, Digumarti and S. Chandra Mohan (2002). *Sports Management.* New Delhi: APH Publishing House. ISBN 81-7648-467-9.

Bhaskara Rao, Digumarti and S.A. Khader (2004). *Problems of Private School Teachers.* New Delhi: Discovery Publishing Corporation. ISBN 81-7141-838-4.

Bhaskara Rao, Digumarti and S.A. Khader (2004). *School Education in India.* New Delhi: Discovery Publishing Corporation. ISBN 81-7141-849-X.

Bhaskara Rao, Digumarti and Sk. Johni Basha (2004). *Teachers' Population Education Awareness.* New Delhi: Discovery Publishing House. ISBN 81-7141-832-5.

Bhaskara Rao, Digumarti, V.V. Rao, V.V. Lakshmi and V.V. Krishna, editors (1999). *Status and Advancement of Women.* New Delhi: APH Publishing Corporation. ISBN 81-7648-169-6.

Appala Naidu, P.Ch., author and Digumarti Bhaskara Rao, editor (2007). *Feedback Methods and Student Performance.* New Delhi: Discovery Publishing House. ISBN 81-8356-284-1.

Babu, P.C., author and Digumarti Bhaskara Rao, editor (2004). *Flowers of Wisdom.* New Delhi: Discovery Publishing House. ISBN 81-7141-695-0.

Bujji Babu, K., author and Digumarti Bhaskara Rao, editor (2007). *Teaching Aptitude of Primary School Teachers.* New Delhi: Sonali Publications. ISBN 81-8411-083-9.

Amala, P.A. and Anupama, P., authors and Digumarti Bhaskara Rao, editor (2004). *History of Education.* New Delhi: Discovery Publishing House. ISBN 81-7141-860-0.

Bhagya Lakshmi, L., Author and Digumarti Bhaskara Rao, editor (2000). *Reading and Comprehension.* New Delhi: Discovery Publishing House. ISBN 81-7141-543-1.

Bhasha, S.A., author and Digumarti Bhaskara Rao, editor (2004). *Methods of Teaching Geography.* New Delhi: Discovery Publishing House. ISBN 81-7141-807-4.

Bhuvaneswara Lakshmi, Gadde, author and Digumarti Bhaskara Rao, editor (2000). *Attitude Towards Science.* New Delhi: Discovery Publishing House. ISBN 81-7141-541-6.

Bhuvaneswara Lakshmi, G., author and Digumarti Bhaskara Rao, editor (2004). *Methods of Teaching Life Science.* New Delhi: Discovery Publishing House. ISBN 81-7141-804-X.

Bhuvaneswara Lakshmi, G. and K. Subba Rao, authors and Digumarti Bhaskara Rao, editor (2004). *Methods of Teaching Biology.* New Delhi: Discovery Publishing House. ISBN 81-7141-914-3.

Bramhaiah, T., author and Digumarti Bhaskara Rao, editor (2008). *Stress of Student Teachers.* New Delhi: Sonali Publications.

Chary, K.V.N.B., author and Digumarti Bhaskara Rao, editor (2006). *Techniques of Teaching Physics.* New Delhi: Sonali Publications. ISBN 81-8411-046-4.

Chowdary, S.B.J.R. and Naga Raju, authors and Digumarti Bhaskara Rao, editor (2004). *Mastery of Teaching Skills.* New Delhi: Discovery Publishing House. ISBN 81-7141-861-9

Dayakara Reddy, V. and Digumarti Bhaskara Rao, editors (2006). *Value-Oriented Education.* New Delhi: Discovery Publishing House. ISBN 81-8356-051-2.

Devraj, T.A.S., author and Digumarti Bhaskara Rao, editor (1997). *Trace Analysis of Uranium and Thorium.* New Delhi: Discovery Publishing House. ISBN 81-7141-375-7.

Durga Rani, K., author and Digumarti Bhaskara Rao, editor (2000). *Educational Aspirations and Scientific Attitudes.* New Delhi: Discovery Publishing House. ISBN 81-7141-555-5.

Dutt, B.S.V. and Digumarti Bhaskara Rao (2001). *Empowering Primary Teachers.* New Delhi: Discovery Publishing House. ISBN 81-7141-615-2.

Dutt, B.S.V., author and Digumarti Bhaskara Rao, editor (2004). *Comparative Education.* New Delhi: Discovery Publishing House. ISBN 81-7141-912-7.

Ediger, Marlow and Digumarti Bhaskara Rao (1996). *Science Curriculum.* New Delhi: Discovery Publishing House. ISBN 81-7141-321-8.

Ediger, Marlow and Digumarti Bhaskara Rao (2000). *Teaching Mathematics Successfully.* New Delhi: Discovery Publishing House. ISBN 81-7141-552-0.

Ediger, Marlow and Digumarti Bhaskara Rao (2001). *Teaching Science Successfully.* New Delhi: Discovery Publishing House. ISBN 81-7141-600-4.

Ediger, Marlow and Digumarti Bhaskara Rao (2001). *Teaching Social Studies Successfully.* New Delhi: Discovery Publishing House. ISBN 81-7141-596-2.

Ediger, Marlow and Digumarti Bhaskara Rao (2002). *Philosophy and Curriculum.* New Delhi: Discovery Publishing House. ISBN 81-7141-631-4.

Ediger, Marlow and Digumarti Bhaskara Rao (2002). *Improving School Administration.* New Delhi: Discovery Publishing House. ISBN 81-7141-633-0.

Ediger, Marlow and Digumarti Bhaskara Rao (2002). *Elementary Curriculum.* New Delhi: Discovery Publishing House. ISBN 81-7141-658-6.

Ediger, Marlow and Digumarti Bhaskara Rao (2003). *Language Arts Curriculum.* New Delhi: Discovery Publishing House. ISBN 81-7141-657-8.

Ediger, Marlow and Digumarti Bhaskara Rao (2003). *Psychology and Curriculum.* New Delhi: Discovery Publishing House. ISBN 81-7141-691-8.

Ediger, Marlow and Digumarti Bhaskara Rao (2003). *Teaching Language Arts Successfully.* New Delhi: Discovery Publishing House. ISBN 81-7141-678-0.

Ediger, Marlow and Digumarti Bhaskara Rao (2003). *School Curriculum and Administration.* New Delhi: Discovery Publishing House. ISBN 81-7141-709-4.

Ediger, Marlow and Digumarti Bhaskara Rao (2003). *Teaching Mathematics in Elementary Schools.* New Delhi: Discovery Publishing House. ISBN 81-7141-687-X.

Ediger, Marlow and Digumarti Bhaskara Rao (2003). *Teaching Science in Elementary Schools.* New Delhi: Discovery Publishing House. ISBN 81-7141-698-5.

Ediger, Marlow and Digumarti Bhaskara Rao (2003). *School Curriculum and Administration.* New Delhi: Discovery Publishing House. ISBN 81-7141-709-4.

Ediger, Marlow and Digumarti Bhaskara Rao (2003). Elementary Curriculum Improvement. New Delhi: Discovery Publishing House. ISBN 81-7141-740-X.

Ediger, Marlow and Digumarti Bhaskara Rao (2004). *School Organisation*. New Delhi: Discovery Publishing House. ISBN 81-7141-843-0.

Ediger, Marlow and Digumarti Bhaskara Rao (2004). *Relevancy in Elementary Curriculum*. New Delhi: Discovery Publishing House. ISBN 81-7141-845-9.

Ediger, Marlow and Digumarti Bhaskara Rao (2005). *Quality School Education*. New Delhi: Discovery Publishing House. ISBN 81-8356-022-9.

Ediger, Marlow and Digumarti Bhaskara Rao (2006). *Successful School Education*. New Delhi: Discovery Publishing House. ISBN 81-8356-054-7.

Ediger, Marlow and Digumarti Bhaskara Rao (2006). *Successful School Administration*. New Delhi: Discovery Publishing House. ISBN 81-8356-046-6.

Ediger, Marlow and Digumarti Bhaskara Rao (2006). *Issues in School Curriculum*. New Delhi: Discovery Publishing House. ISBN 81-8356-052-0.

Ediger, Marlow and Digumarti Bhaskara Rao (2006). *Community College – Curriculum and Teaching*. New Delhi: Discovery Publishing House. ISBN 81-8356-053-9.

Ediger, Marlow and Digumarti Bhaskara Rao (2006). *Administration of Schools*. New Delhi: Discovery Publishing House. ISBN 81-8356-244-2.

Ediger, Marlow and Digumarti Bhaskara Rao (2006). *Reading Curriculum and Instruction*. New Delhi: Discovery Publishing House. ISBN 81-8356-266-3.

Ediger, Marlow and Digumarti Bhaskara Rao (2006). *Curriculum Organisation*. New Delhi: Discovery Publishing House. ISBN 81-8356-205-1.

Ediger, Marlow and Digumarti Bhaskara Rao (2006). *Curriculum of School Subjects*. New Delhi: Discovery Publishing House. ISBN 81-8356-207-8.

Ediger, Marlow, B.S.V. Dutt and Digumarti Bhaskara Rao (2003). *Teaching English Successfully.* New Delhi: Discovery Publishing House. ISBN 81-7141-707-8.

Ediger, Marlow and Digumarti Bhaskara Rao (2007). *School Science Education.* New Delhi: Discovery Publishing House. ISBN 81-8356-352-X.

Ediger, Marlow and Digumarti Bhaskara Rao (2007). *Language Arts Education.* New Delhi: Discovery Publishing House. ISBN 81-8356-333-3.

Elizabeth, M.E.S., author and Digumarti Bhaskara Rao, editor (2004). *Methods of Teaching English.* New Delhi: Discovery Publishing House. ISBN 81-7141-809-0.

Elizabeth, M.E.S., author and Digumarti Bhaskara Rao, editor (2004). *Acquisition of English Vocabulary.* New Delhi: Discovery Publishing House. ISBN 81-8356-075-X.

Fatima, Sk. author and Digumarti Bhaskara Rao, editor (2007). *Reasoning Ability of School Students.* New Delhi: Discovery Publishing House. ISBN 81-8356-330-9.

Fatima, Sk. and Digumarti Bhaskara Rao (2008). *Reasoning Ability of Adolescent Students.* New Delhi: Sonali Publications. ISBN 978-81-8356-315-4.

Gopala Krishna, M., author and Digumarti Bhaskara Rao, editor (2007). *Techniques of Teaching Physical Education.* New Delhi: Sonali Publications. ISBN 81-8411-044-8.

Gopala Krishna, M., author and Digumarti Bhaskara Rao, editor (2007). *Techniques of Teaching Education.* New Delhi: Sonali Publications. ISBN 81-8411-062-6.

Harshitha, Digumarthi, author and Digumarti Bhaskara Rao, editor (2004). *Methods of Teaching Information Technology.* New Delhi: Discovery Publishing House. ISBN 81-7141-805-8.

Harshitha, Digumarthi, author and Digumarti Bhaskara Rao, editor (2007). *Techniques of Teaching Computer Science.* New Delhi: Sonali Publications. ISBN 81-8411-036-7.

Indira Devi, author and J. Prasanth Kumar and Digumarti Bhaskara Rao, editors (2004). *Values in Language Text Books*. New Delhi: Discovery Publishing House. ISBN 81-7141-833-3.

Jalaja Kumari, C., author and Digumarti Bhaskara Rao, editor (2004). *Methods of Teaching Educational Technology*. New Delhi: Discovery Publishing House. ISBN 81-7141-810-4.

Jalaja Kumari, C., author and Digumarti Bhaskara Rao, editor (2007). *Job Satisfaction of Teachers*. New Delhi: Discovery Publishing House. ISBN 81-8356-329-5.

Janardhan Reddy, B., author and Digumarti Bhaskara Rao, editor (2006). *Techniques of Teaching Sociology*. New Delhi: Sonali Publications. ISBN 81-8411-042-1.

Jayalakshmi, M., author and Digumarti Bhaskara Rao, editor (2008). *Microteaching and Prospective Teachers*. New Delhi: Discovery Publishing House. ISBN 978-81-8356-375-8.

Jayasree, K., author and Digumarti Bhaskara Rao, editor (1999). *Correlates of Socialisation*. New Delhi: Discovery Publishing House. ISBN 81-7141-517-2.

Jayasree, K., author and Digumarti Bhaskara Rao, editor (2004). *Methods of Teaching Science*. New Delhi: Discovery Publishing House. ISBN 81-7141-801-5.

John Babu, C., author and T.J.R. Prasad, G.M. Madhukar and Digumarti Bhaskara Rao, editors (2004). *Problem Solving in Mathematics*. New Delhi: APH Publishing Corporation. ISBN 81-7648-273-0.

Joseph Raju, B and G.A. Anitha, authors and Digumarti Bhaskara Rao, editor (2004). *Population Education*. New Delhi: Sonali Publications. ISBN 81-88836-31-3.

Lalitha, T., author and K.S. Prabhakaram, D.S.N. Sastry and Digumarti Bhaskara Rao, editors (2004). *Educational Philosophic Beliefs*. New Delhi: Discovery Publishing House. ISBN 81-7141-765-5.

Krishna, G., author and Digumarti Bhaskara Rao, editor (2006). *Techniques of Teaching Physical Education.* New Delhi: Discovery Publishing House. ISBN 81-8411-044-8.

Kumar Raja, G., author and Digumarti Bhaskara Rao, editor (2007). *Principles of Primary School.* New Delhi: Sonali Publications. ISBN 81-8411-054-5.

Lakshmi Kumari, V., author and Digumarti Bhaskara Rao, editor (2006). *Techniques of Teaching Home Science.* New Delhi: Discovery Publishing House. ISBN 81-8411-048-0.

Madhava, K., author and Digumarti Bhaskara Rao, editor (2008). *Personality of Adolescent Students.* New Delhi: Discovery Publishing House. ISBN 978-81-8356-262-1.

Madhu Bala, Jampala, author and Digumarti Bhaskara Rao, editor (2004). *Methods of Teaching Exceptional Children.* New Delhi: Discovery Publishing House. ISBN 81-7141-802-3.

Madhu Bala, Jampala, author and Digumarti Bhaskara Rao, editor (2007). *Adjustment Problems of Hearing Impaired.* New Delhi: Discovery Publishing House. ISBN 81-7141-831-7.

Marja, Talvi and Digumarti Bhaskara Rao, editors (1996). *Educational Leadership and Social Changes.* New Delhi: Discovery Publishing House. ISBN 81-7141-320-X.

Mohana Sundari, C., author and B. Prasad Babu and Digumarti Bhaskara Rao, editors (2008). *Stress among Pregnant Women* New Delhi: Discovery Publishing House. ISBN 978-81-8356-316-1.

Naga Kumari, U., author and Digumarti Bhaskara Rao, editor (2008). *Science Process Skills of School Students.* New Delhi: Discovery Publishing House. ISBN 978-81-8356-263-8.

Nageswara Rao, S. and M. Srihari, authors and Digumarti Bhaskara Rao, editor (2004). *Guidance and Counselling.* New Delhi: Discovery Publishing House. ISBN 81-7141-840-6.

Nageswara Rao, S., author and Digumarti Bhaskara Rao, editor (2006). *Techniques of Teaching Psychology.* New Delhi: Discovery Publishing House. ISBN 81-8411-040-5.

Nageswara Rao, S. and P. Sridhar, authors and Digumarti Bhaskara Rao, editor (2004). *Methods and Techniques of Teaching.* New Delhi: Sonali Publications. ISBN 81-88836-33-8.

Nirmala Jyothi, M., author and Digumarti Bhaskara Rao, editor (2003). *Non-detention System in School Education.* New Delhi: Discovery Publishing House. ISBN 81-7141-654-3.

Padma Tulasi, G., author and Digumarti Bhaskara Rao, editor (2004). *Methods of Teaching Elementary Science.* New Delhi: Discovery Publishing House. ISBN 81-7141-871-6.

Pala Prasada Rao, V., author and K. N. Rani and D. Bhaskara Rao, editors (2004).*India Pakistan: Partition Perspectives in Indo English Novels.* New Delhi: Discovery Publishing House. ISBN 81-7141-871-6.

Pala Prasada Rao, V., author and D. Bhaskara Rao, editors (2008). *Functioning of Autonomous Colleges.* New Delhi: Discovery Publishing House. ISBN 978-81-8356-258-4.

Pitchi Reddy, M., author and Digumarti Bhaskara Rao, editor (2007). *Techniques of Teaching Social Sciences.* New Delhi: Sonali Publications. ISBN 81-8411-066-X.

Prabhakaram, K.S., author and Digumarti Bhaskara Rao, editor (1998). *Concept Attainment Model in Mathematics Teaching.* New Delhi: Discovery Publishing House. ISBN 81-7141-424-9.

Prasad Babu, B., author and P. Madhu and Digumarti Bhaskara Rao, editors (2006). *Psychological Adjustment and Well-being.* New Delhi: Discovery Publishing House. ISBN 81-8356-204-3.

Prasad Babu, B., author and M.V.R. Raju and Digumarti Bhaskara Rao, editors (2006). *Behavioural Problems of School Children.* New Delhi: Discovery Publishing House. ISBN 81-8356-206-X.

Prasanth Kumar, J., author and Digumarti Bhaskara Rao, editor (1998). *Effectiveness of Distance Education System*. New Delhi: Discovery Publishing House. ISBN 81-7141-437-0.

Prasanth Kumar, J., author and Digumarti Bhaskara Rao, editor (2004). *Methods of Teaching Civics*. New Delhi: Discovery Publishing House. ISBN 81-7141-806-6.

Prasanth Kumar, J., author and G. Sundara Rao and Digumarti Bhaskara Rao, editors (2000). *Open University Student Support Services*. New Delhi: Discovery Publishing House. ISBN 81-7141-550-4.

Praveena, P., author and Digumarti Bhaskara Rao, editor (2009). *Adjustment and Teacher Educators*. New Delhi: Discovery Publishing House.

Raja Kumari, M.A. and D.R.S. Sundari, authors and Digumarti Bhaskara Rao, editor (2004). *Special Education*. New Delhi: Discovery Publishing House. ISBN 81-7141-846-5.

Raja Kumari, M.A. and D.R.S. Sundari, authors and Digumarti Bhaskara Rao, editor (2004). *Methods of Teaching Educational Psychology*. New Delhi: Discovery Publishing House. ISBN 81-7141-820-1.

Rajeswari, S. M., author and T. Santhanam, B. Prasad Babu and Digumarti Bhaskara Rao, editors (2008). *Stress and Attitude of Women Teachers*. New Delhi: Discovery Publishing House. ISBN 978-81-8356-324-6.

Ramatulasamma, K., author and Digumarti Bhaskara Rao, editor (2002). *Job Satisfaction of Teacher Educators*. New Delhi: Discovery Publishing House. ISBN 81-7141-655-1.

Rama Krishnaiah, D., author and Digumarti Bhaskara Rao, editor (1998). *Job Satisfaction of College Teachers*. New Delhi: Discovery Publishing House. ISBN 81-7141-438-9.

Rama Kumar Ratnam, M.V., author and Digumarti Bhaskara Rao, editor (1998). *Dukkha: Suffering in Early Buddhism*. New Delhi: Discovery Publishing House. ISBN 81-7141-653-5.

Rama Krishna Prasad and P. Vide Sagar, authors and Digumarti Bhaskara Rao, editor (2004). *Methods of Teaching Physical Education.* New Delhi: Discovery Publishing House. ISBN 81-7141-868-6.

Rama Seshaiah, P. author and Digumarti Bhaskara Rao, editor (2004). *Methods of Teaching Home Science.* New Delhi: Discovery Publishing House. ISBN 81-7141-916-X.

Rama Swamy, K., author and Digumarti Bhaskara Rao, editor (2007). *Techniques of Teaching Environmental Science.* New Delhi: Sonali Publications. ISBN 81-8411-035-9.

Ramesh, A.R., author and Digumarti Bhaskara Rao, editor (2006). *Techniques of Teaching Commerce.* New Delhi: Sonali Publications. ISBN 81-8411-043-X.

Ramesh, Ghanta and Digumarti Bhaskara Rao, editors (1998). *Environmental Education: Problems and Prospects.* New Delhi: Discovery Publishing House. ISBN 81-7141-423-0.

Ranga Rao, B., author and Digumarti Bhaskara Rao, editor (2007). *Techniques of Teaching Economics.* New Delhi: Sonali Publications. ISBN 81-8411-056-1.

Ranga Rao, R., author and Digumarti Bhaskara Rao, editor (2004). *Methods of Teacher Teaching.* New Delhi: Discovery Publishing House. ISBN 81-7141-812-0.

Rani, S.S., author and Digumarti Bhaskara Rao, editor (2006). *Techniques of Teaching Botany.* New Delhi: Discovery Publishing House. ISBN 81-8411-037-5.

Rathaiah, Lavu and Digumarti Bhaskara Rao, editors (1996), *International Innovations in Education.* New Delhi: Discovery Publishing House. ISBN 81-7141-359-5.

Rathaiah, Lavu and Digumarti Bhaskara Rao (1997). *Achievement Correlates.* New Delhi: Discovery Publishing House. ISBN 81-7141-385-4.

Ravi Krishna, M., author and Digumarti Bhaskara Rao, editor (2004). *Examination System.* New Delhi: Discovery Publishing House. ISBN 81-7141-824-4.

Ravi Kumar, M., author and Digumarti Bhaskara Rao, editor (2004). *Methods of Teaching Computer Science*. New Delhi: Discovery Publishing House. ISBN 81-7141-823-6.

Roja Ramani, V., author and Digumarti Bhaskara Rao, editor (2009). *Frustration of Prospective Teachers*. New Delhi: Discovery Publishing House. ISBN 978-81-8356-377-2.

Rudramamba, B., author and Digumarti Bhaskara Rao, editor (2003). *Problems of Teaching*. New Delhi: APH Publishing Corporation. ISBN 81-7648-462-8.

Rudramamba, B. and V. Lakshmi Kumari, authors and Digumarti Bhaskara Rao, editor (2004). *Methods of Teaching Economics*. New Delhi: Discovery Publishing House. ISBN 81-7141-900-3.

Sambasiva Rao, P., author and Digumarti Bhaskara Rao, editor (2007). *Techniques of Teaching Psychology*. New Delhi: Sonali Publications. ISBN 81-8411-040-5.

Sanjeeva Rao, P.C., author and Digumarti Bhaskara Rao, editor (1996). *A Text Book of Geology*. New Delhi: Discovery Publishing House. ISBN 81-7141-313-7.

Santhanam, T., B. Prasad Babu and S. Sugandhi, authors and Digumarti Bhaskara Rao, editor (2007). *Children with Learning Disabilities*. New Delhi: Sonali Publications. ISBN 81-8411-077-4.

Santhanam, T., B. Prasad Babu and S. Sugandhi, authors and Digumarti Bhaskara Rao, editor (2008). *Learning Disabilities and Remedial Programmes*. New Delhi: Discovery Publishing House. ISBN 978-81-8356-257-7.

Sarala, M.M.O., author and Digumarti Bhaskara Rao, editor (2006). *Techniques of Teaching English*. New Delhi: Sonali Publications. ISBN 81-8411-047-2.

Sashibhushan Goud, K, author and Digumarti Bhaskara Rao, editor (2009). *Attitude of Teachers towards Computers*. New Delhi: Discovery Publishing House.

Satya Narayana, G., author and Digumarti Bhaskara Rao, editor (2008). *Attitude towards Social Studies and Achievement in Social Studies*. New Delhi: Discovery Publishing House. ISBN 978-81-8356-261-4.

Satya Narayana, V., author and Digumarti Bhaskara Rao, editor (2001). *Physical Education, Social Attitudes and Leadership Qualities*. New Delhi: Discovery Publishing House. ISBN 81-7141-593-8.

Satya Narayana, P.V.V. and G. Krishna, authors and Digumarti Bhaskara Rao, editor (2004). *Curriculum Development and Management*. New Delhi: Discovery Publishing House. ISBN 81-7141-813-9.

Shamsuddin, Sk. and V. Dayakara Reddy, authors and Digumarti Bhaskara Rao, editor (2007). *Values and Academic Achievement*. New Delhi: Discovery Publishing House. ISBN 81-8356-283-3.

Singh, Y.C., author and Digumarti Bhaskara Rao, editor (2006). *Techniques of Teaching Science*. New Delhi: Sonali Publications. ISBN 81-8411-041-3.

Sirisha Rani, S., author and Digumarti Bhaskara Rao, editor (2007). *Techniques of Teaching Botany*. New Delhi: Sonali Publications. ISBN 81-8411-037-5.

Sivaratnam Reddy, M., author and Digumarti Bhaskara Rao, editor (2004). *Creativity in College Students*. New Delhi: Discovery Publishing House. ISBN 81-7141-697-7.

Siva Lakshmi, G.V. and G.L. Subbaiah, authors and Digumarti Bhaskara Rao, editor (2004). *Methods of Teaching Environmental Science*. New Delhi: Discovery Publishing House. ISBN 81-7141-839-2.

Srinivas, G. and Digumarti Bhaskara Rao (2007). *Anxiety of Prospective Teachers*. New Delhi: Sonali Publications. ISBN 81-8411-084-7.

Srinivas, M. and I. Prasada Rao, authors and Digumarti Bhaskara Rao, editor (2004). *Methods of Teaching History*. New Delhi: Discovery Publishing House. ISBN 81-7141-803-1.

Srinivas Rao, P., author and Digumarti Bhaskara Rao, editor (2007). *Principles of Secondary School.* New Delhi: Sonali Publications. ISBN 81-8411-058-8.

Srinivasulu Reddy, M. and K.R.S. Sambasiva Rao, authors and Digumarti Bhaskara Rao, editor (1999). *A Text Book of Aquaculture.* New Delhi: Discovery Publishing House. ISBN 81-7141-482-6.

Srinivasa Rao, Mandalapu, author and Digumarti Bhaskara Rao, editor (2003). *Achievement Motivation and Achievement in Mathematics.* New Delhi: Discovery Publishing House. ISBN 81-7141-674-8.

Srihari, M., author and Digumarti Bhaskara Rao, editor (2003). *Values of Prospective Teachers.* New Delhi: Discovery Publishing House. ISBN 81-8356-328-7.

Subba Rao, K., author and Digumarti Bhaskara Rao, editor (2007). *School Education Policy.* New Delhi: Discovery Publishing House. ISBN 81-8356-285-X.

Subba Rao, K., author and Digumarti Bhaskara Rao, editor (2007). *Educational Planning.* New Delhi: Sonali Publications. ISBN 81-8411-053-7.

Sudhakar Reddy, Y., author and Digumarti Bhaskara Rao, editor (2003). *Creativity in Adolescents.* New Delhi: Discovery Publishing House. ISBN 81-7141-659-4.

Sunil Kumar, K. and K. Rama Krishana, authors and Digumarti Bhaskara Rao, editor (2004). *Methods of Teaching Chemistry.* New Delhi: Discovery Publishing House. ISBN 81-7141-913-5.

Suneetha, G., author and Digumarti Bhaskara Rao, editor (2004). *Environmental Awareness of School Students.* New Delhi: Sonali Publications. ISBN 81-8411-085-5.

Sunita, E. and R. Sambasiva Rao, authors and Digumarti Bhaskara Rao, editor (2004). *Methods of Teaching Mathematics.* New Delhi: Discovery Publishing House. ISBN 81-7141-915-1.

Suresh, K., author and Digumarti Bhaskara Rao, editor (2008). *Social Intelligence of Student Teachers*. New Delhi: Discovry Publishing House. ISBN 978-81-8356-374-1.

Surya Madhava, I., author and Digumarti Bhaskara Rao, editor (2006). *Techniques of Teaching Geography*. New Delhi: Discovery Publishing House. ISBN 81-8411-034-0.

Surya Madhava, I., author and Digumarti Bhaskara Rao, editor (2007). *Techniques of Teaching Political Science*. New Delhi: Discovery Publishing House. ISBN 81-8411-061-8.

Suvarna Raju, T.J.M., author and M.V.R. Raju, B. Prasad Babu and Digumarti Bhaskara Rao, editors (2009). *Personality and Adjustment of University Hostel Students*. New Delhi: Discovery Publishing House. ISBN 978-81-8356-424-3.

Swamy, K.R., author and Digumarti Bhaskara Rao, editor (2006). *Techniques of Teaching Environmental Science*. New Delhi: Discovery Publishing House. ISBN 81-8411-035-9.

Swarna Jyothi, K., author and Digumarti Bhaskara Rao, editor (2007). *Educational Research*. New Delhi: Sonali Publications. ISBN 81-8411-063-4.

Swarna Latha, C.D., and Digumarti Bhaskara Rao, editors (2006). *Encyclopaedia of Biotechnology*, 5 volumes. New Delhi: Discovery Publishing House. ISBN 81-8356-168-3.

Swarupa Rani, T. and J.R. Priyadarshini, authors and Digumarti Bhaskara Rao, editor (2004). *Educational Measurement and Evaluation*. New Delhi: Discovery Publishing House. ISBN 81-7141-859-7.

Vanaja, M., author and Digumarti Bhaskara Rao, editor (1999). *Inquiry Training Model*. New Delhi: Discovery Publishing House. ISBN 81-7141-515-6.

Vanaja, M., author and Digumarti Bhaskara Rao, editor (2004). *Methods of Teaching Physics*. New Delhi: Discovery Publishing House. ISBN 81-7141-867-8.

Valeri V. Koustiouk, author and Digumarti Bhaskara Rao, editor (2002). *A Text Book of Cryogenics*. New Delhi: Discovery Publishing House. ISBN 81-7141-642-X.

Vamsi Krishna, V., author and Digumarti Bhaskara Rao, editor (2004). *School Psychology*. New Delhi: Discovery Publishing House. ISBN 81-7141-880-5.

Veena Kumari, Balusu and Digumarti Bhaskara Rao (1996). *Operation Black Board*. New Delhi: APH Publishing Corporation. ISBN 81-7024-711-X.

Veena Kumari, Balusu, author and Digumarti Bhaskara Rao, editor (2004). *Methods of Teaching Social Studies*. New Delhi: Discovery Publishing House. ISBN 81-7141-899-6.

Veena Kumari, Balusu, author and Digumarti Bhaskara Rao, editor (2000). *Psycho-Social Correlates of Achievement*. New Delhi: Discovery Publishing House. ISBN 81-7141-547-4.

Venkata Rao, B., author and Digumarti Bhaskara Rao, editor (2007). *Techniques of Teaching Chemistry*. New Delhi: Sonali Publications. ISBN 81-8411-057-X.

Venkata Rao, P. and Digumarti Bhaskara Rao (1989). *A Text Book of Zoology – Junior Intermediate*. Guntur: Vignan Publishers.

Venkata Rao, P. and Digumarti Bhaskara Rao (1989). *A Text Book of Zoology – Senior Intermediate*. Guntur: Vignan Publishers.

Venkateswara Rao, V., author and Digumarti Bhaskara Rao, editor (2004). *Problems of Education*. New Delhi: Discovery Publishing House. ISBN 81-7141-841-4.

Venkateswara Rao, V., V. Vijaya Lakshmi and V. Vamsi Krishna, authors and Digumarti Bhaskara Rao, editor (2004). *Education For All*. New Delhi: Sonali Publications. ISBN 81-88836-30-3.

Venkateswara Rao, V., V. Vijaya Lakshmi and V. Vamsi Krishna, authors and Digumarti Bhaskara Rao, editor (2004). *Education in India*. New Delhi: Sonali Publications. ISBN 81-88836-858-9.

Venkateswara Reddy, L. and Narayana, M. L., authors and Digumarti Bhaskara Rao, editor (2004). *Education for Dalits*. New Delhi: Discovery Publishing House. ISBN 81-7141-872-4.

Venkateswara Reddy, L. and Narayana, M. L, authors and Digumarti Bhaskara Rao, editor (2004). *Methods of Teaching Rural Sociology*. New Delhi: Discovery Publishing House. ISBN 81-7141-811-2.

Venkateswarlu, K. and S.J. Basha, authors and Digumarti Bhaskara Rao, editor (2004). *Methods of Teaching Commerce*. New Delhi: Discovery Publishing House. ISBN 81-7141-808-2.

Venugopala Rao, K., author and Digumarti Bhaskara Rao, editor (2000). *Teacher Morale in Secondary Schools*. New Delhi: Discovery Publishing House. ISBN 81-7141-551-2.

Venugopala Rao, K., author and Digumarti Bhaskara Rao, editor (2007). *Techniques of Teaching History*. New Delhi: Sonali Publications. ISBN 81-8411-059-6.

Vidya, C., author and Digumarti Bhaskara Rao, editor (1996). *A Text Book of Nutrition*. New Delhi: Discovery Publishing House. ISBN 81-7141-309-9.

Vimala, T.D., B. Prasad Babu and Digumarti Bhaskara Rao, editors (2007). *Stress, Coping and Management*. New Delhi: Sonali Publications. ISBN 81-8411-086-3.

Vijaya Bharathi, D., author and Digumarti Bhaskara Rao, editor (2000). *Educational Philosophies of Swami Vivekananda and John Dewey*. New Delhi: APH Publishing House. ISBN 81-7648-309-9.

Vijaya Bharathi, D., author and Digumarti Bhaskara Rao, editor (2005). *Educational Philosophy of John Dewey*. New Delhi: Discovery Publishing House. ISBN 81-8356-024-5.

Vijaya Bharathi, D., author and Digumarti Bhaskara Rao, editor (2005). *Educational Philosophy of Swami Vivekananda*. New Delhi: Discovery Publishing House. ISBN 81-8356-023-7.

Vijaya Lakshmi, D., author and Digumarti Bhaskara Rao, editor (2004) *Basic Education*. New Delhi: Discovery Publishing House. ISBN 81-7141-881-3.

Vijaya Lakshmi, V., author and Digumarti Bhaskara Rao, editor (2006). *Techniques of Teaching Music*. New Delhi: Discovery Publishing House. ISBN 81-8411-038-3.

Vijaya Kumar, S.J., author and Digumarti Bhaskara Rao, editor (2006). *Techniques of Teaching Mathematics*. New Delhi: Sonali Publications. ISBN 81-8411-039-1.

Visalakshi, V., author and Digumarti Bhaskara Rao, editor (2006). *Techniques of Teaching Biology*. New Delhi: Sonali Publications. ISBN 81-8411-045-6.

Visalakshi, V., author and Digumarti Bhaskara Rao, editor (2007). *Techniques of Teaching Zoology*. New Delhi: Sonali Publications. ISBN 81-8411-055-3.

Books in Telugu Language

Bhaskara Rao, Digumarti (1986). *Dhrushya Sravana Bodhanapakaranalu* (Audio Visual Teaching Aids). Guntur: Nagarjuna Publishers.

Bhaskara Rao, Digumarti (1993). *Jeevasastra Bodhana* (Teaching of Biology). Guntur: Nagarjuna Publishers.

Bhaskara Rao, Digumarti (1995). *Vignanasastra Bodhana* (Teaching of science) Guntur: Nagarjuna Publishers.

Bhaskara Rao, Digumarti (1997). *Vidya Manovignana Sastram* (Educational Psychology). Guntur: Creative Press.

Bhaskara Rao, Digumarti (1998). *DSC Study Material*. Guntur: Nagarjuna Publishers.

Bhaskara Rao, Digumarti (1998). *Upadhyayudu Vidya*. (Teacher and Education) Guntur: Nagarjuna Publishers.

Bhaskara Rao, Digumarti (1998). *Vidya Drukpadalu* (Perspectives of Education). Guntur: Nagarjuna Publishers.

Bhaskara Rao, Digumarti (1999). *EdCET Teaching Aptitude.* Guntur: Nagarjuna Publishers.

Bhaskara Rao, Digumarti (2001). *Bharata Samajamulo Upadyayudu Vidhya* (Teacher and Education in Emerging Indian Society). Guntur: Sri Nagarjuna Publishers.

Bhaskara Rao, Digumarti (2001). *Bhoutika Sastra Bodhana Padhatulu* (Methods of Teaching Physical Science). Guntur: Sri Nagarjuna Publishers.

Bhaskara Rao, Digumarti (2001). *Jeeva Sastra Bodhana Padhatulu* (Methods of Teaching Biology).Guntur: Sri Nagarjuna Publishers.

Bhaskara Rao, Digumarti (2001). *Vidya Manovignana Sastram* (Educational Psychology). Guntur: Sri Nagarjuna Publishers.

Bhaskara Rao, Digumarti and M. Srihari (2009). *Vardhamana Desamlo Vidya* (Education in Emerging India). Guntur: Sri Nagarjuna Publishers.

Bhaskara Rao, Digumarti and B. Prasad Babu (2009). *Vidya Manovignana Sastram* (Educational Psychology). Guntur: Sri Nagarjuna Publishers.

Bhaskara Rao, Digumarti and K. Subba Rao (2009). *Elementary Vidya, Pranalika Rachana, Yajamanyam, Upadyaya Vidhulu* (Elementary Education, Planning, Management and Teacher Functions). Guntur: Sri Nagarjuna Publishers.

Bhaskara Rao, Digumarti and B. Prasad Babu (2009). *Pradhamika Vidhya mariyu Vileena Vidhyaya Dhrukpadhalu* (Perspectives in Primary Education and Inclusive Education). Guntur: Sri Nagarjuna Publishers.

Bhaskara Rao, Digumarti and A. Jagadish (2009). *Vignanasastra Bodhana Padhatulu* (Methods of Teaching Science). Guntur: Sri Nagarjuna Publishers.

Gopala Krishna, G., A. Rama Krishna, K. Subba Rao and Bhaskara Rao, Digumarti (2004). *Jeevasashtra Bodhana Padhatulu* (Methods of Teaching of Biological science). Guntur: Sri Nagarjuna Publishers.

Krishna Murthy, V., K.S. Sudheer Reddy and Digumarti Bhaskara Rao (2004). *Vidya Manovignana Sastra Adharalu* (Foundations of Educational Psychology). Guntur: Sri Nagarjuna Publishers.

Lalini, V., V. Dayakara Reddy, M. Srihari and Digumarti Bhaskara Rao (2004). *Vidya Adharalu* (Foundations of Education). Guntur: Sri Nagarjuna Publishers.

Subba Rao, K.P., P. Ayodhya and Digumarti Bhaskara Rao (2004). *Patasala Yajamanyam – Vidhya Vyavasthalu* (School Management and Systems of Education). Guntur: Sri Nagarjuna Publishers.

Sudhakar, V., B. Ravindra Babu, D.S. Kumar and Digumarti Bhaskara Rao (2004). *Vidya Sanketika Sastram - Computer Vidhya* (Educational Technology and Computer Education). Guntur: Sri Nagarjuna Publishers.

Index

❑❑❑